Inspiration from my Travels

Inspiration from my Travels

An Immigrant's Eyes on the World: A Memoir

Nalini Juthani

INSPIRATION FROM MY TRAVELS
AN IMMIGRANT'S EYES ON THE WORLD: A MEMOIR

iUniverse books may be ordered through booksellers or by contacting:

iUniverse
1663 Liberty Drive
Bloomington, IN 47403
www.iuniverse.com
1-800-Authors (1-800-288-4677)

ISBN: 978-1-5320-4109-9 (sc)
ISBN: 978-1-5320-4108-2 (e)

Library of Congress Control Number: 2018900565

Print information available on the last page.

iUniverse rev. date: 03/26/2018

For My Husband
Viren

Children
Manisha, Kapila, Viral

And

Our Grandchildren
Ishani, Shaan, Kush, Piya, Kayshar

Contents

List of Illustrations

A Room with a View

Author's Note

As I started to write this book, I realized that there is a running theme that connects all my travels throughout the seven continents of the world. Meeting new people and bonding with the people I knew, making meaningful relationships, learning about their culture, capturing and preserving memories through photography, learning about the history and evolution of each place, the food they ate and the food we could eat or not eat because of our vegetarian food choices, inspired me and made my life richer. Each chapter has a story to tell about the innovative, inspiring and engaging experiences I had in my travels, and I hope some of this may inspire you, if anything, at least get up and travel, and never stop creating new chapters for yourself. You set the limit.

I have enjoyed the process of writing because it has given me an opportunity to walk down the memory lane and to revisit and reflect upon the experiences I had during my travels. Each essay is accompanied by photographs that have captured my underlying mood at that time.

Acknowledgements

I want to acknowledge the people who I encountered on my journey through my travels. My late uncle Jay Gandhi, an author himself, inspired me to write about my experiences which led me to write this book. Although he did not live long enough to read this book, my gratitude goes to him for his support and encouragement. I want to thank my travel partners, my husband, Viren, my three children Manisha, Kapila and Viral who encouraged me to tell stories about my travels.

I want to thank my editor, Carlos Henri-Ferré, who read each story and helped me expand them in my own voice. He listened to these stories with great interest and encouraged me. He offered me new insights into making this book more interesting to people who do not know me. Finally, he said which was very touching to me, "Dr. Juthani, what can I say? You have inspired me to travel, I am on my way!"

I dedicate this book to my grandchildren, Ishani, Shaan, Kush, Piya and Kayshar with a hope that someday they will be inspired to travel the world, learn from their experiences and share their own to enrich their lives. On this journey of life, I was fortunate to travel the world and learn life's valuable lessons.

I want to thank my friend, Bernice Gottlicb whose ideas are unique in many ways. They inspired me to write this second memoir.

Lastly, I quote an unknown author:

Everyone is my teacher, Some I seek, Some I subconsciously attract.

Often I learn simply by observing others.

Some may be completely unaware that I am learning from them, yet I bow deeply in gratitude. This is how I feel about Bernice Gottlieb.

My Dream Land: Kashmir

As a child, my family did not travel for pleasure. Bombay was our home, our confined space. When we did travel, we went to visit our relatives over the school holidays or to religious pilgrimage sites. At most, and rarely, when someone was recovering from a serious medical illness or emotional breakdown, we would take the ailing family member to a *hill station*, or mountainous resort town—if we could afford it—to get away from the daily stressors in Bombay and change climates. We went away to get away: it was an escape.

Throughout my childhood, I accompanied my grandmother on visits to *Rajkot, Manavadar,* and *Limbuda* – all located in the state of Gujarat, India. My grandmother's brothers and their families lived there, and we all looked forward to spending time together over these summer vacations. But, I longed to experience more; I wondered what else was out there beyond the limits I began to see. I began to look for opportunities.

I first experienced *wanderlust* when I was fifteen years old. My all-girls high school in Mumbai sponsored a trip to Kashmir using a tour company. I had never travelled independently without a family member, and to put it simply, this was appealing, very appealing. I could finally expand those boundaries, and I began to learn about myself, that boundaries, limitations, any hold-up, there is always a way around, and I will find it. Now the boundary was convincing my traditional family, and of course paying for it.

I came home from school one day with an announcement of, and an itinerary for, the school trip, unabashedly revealing my intentions. The itinerary showed that we would travel by train, stay in student hostels or hotels, and do some sightseeing. One of our teachers was assigned to accompany twelve girls from my high school.

One morning, the principal met me in the hallway and said, "You are going on this trip, right?" I hesitated to answer, knowing that my mother, grandfather, and grandmother would have serious reservations about allowing me to travel without family supervision. A fifteen year-old-girl, alone, in India, is traveling. At that time, a pipe dream.

From the time that my father passed away when I was five years old, my maternal grandparents had taken me, my mother, and my sister in to live with them. My maternal grandparents were my guardians, and I knew they wanted the best for me. But on the other hand, I wanted some independence, and I really wanted to take this school trip, real independence. No cell phones or internet, this was getting away. The thought of travelling with a group of friends was exciting to me, but I needed permission and money. My only hope was that if I could present this school trip to my paternal grandfather, who I called *"Dadaji,"* to get his permission for this trip, and of course the help.

Dadaji was a stern-looking, highly intellectual man. As an attorney, trained during the era in which India was part of the British Empire, Dadaji was the first one in our community to be in the legal profession. He was feared by most of my family members. However, he believed in me, and supported my somewhat unconventional—at least for a woman in my family at the time—ambitions. He took a keen interest in my upbringing, my education, and my desires.

Although we did not live with Dadaji, he was not that far. He visited me every day and looked over my homework, stressing the importance of education and developing my intellect. Education is the one thing people cannot take away from you. On Sundays we went to his home, a *trip* of some sorts. He would ask me to read aloud "The Times of India," an English newspaper. He taught me to speak "loud and clear" (a lesson I would carry with me throughout my life and pass on to my children and grandchildren) and corrected my pronunciation whenever it needed correction. He had high expectations from me and wanted me to be the best at everything I did.

One evening when he was visiting me, I summoned the courage to talk to him about the upcoming school trip. He responded with a big smile and said, "You must go!" "I will pay for the trip, and you will write to me from every place you visit." This was a relief. He encouraged me to do things that others, especially girls in my family, had not done. I was thrilled. Before I even signed up for the trip, Dadaji was already in planning mode. Needless to say, he had the veto power in the family regarding most decisions that concerned me, my own personal guardian, the father figure I needed. Dadaji's protection, and really influence, as it was, shaped the independent adventurer I am today. Perhaps it was his time in British India, or becoming a man of the law, probably the combination of both. But whatever it was, his vision of my future became the vision of my future. Colonialism or independence, he was a man ahead of his time.

After discussions with my maternal grandparents and my mother—and through their ensuing hesitations, I prevailed victoriously—I was finally signed up to go on this trip. My best friend, Amta, also was set to go and we were excited to have our first *true* independent adventure. I do not think we expected anything, other than seeing beyond the confines of our rearing.

As we began planning for the trip, Dadaji bought me a camera. He told me that I should tell him all about the trip through the photos that I took. I had never held a camera in my hands, let alone owned one. It was a big black box. I learned its features, but felt nervous about the task ahead of me. I was going out there on my own. Sure, we were in a safe and trusted program, but that was not on our minds, we were going on adventures like the stories we read and heard.

Finally, the day that we would begin our adventure arrived. We took a train as a group, accompanied by our teacher. My entire family came to the train station to see us off. We all got on the train and hung out from the windows to have a last glimpse of our family members. Dadaji yelled loudly: "Don't forget to write letters!" His voice quivered as he yelled. He must have had the same angst that my mother and my maternal grandparents felt, but overcame that uneasy feeling to let me go. I nodded "yes," and became tearful as the train set in motion. I was going to be away from home for two weeks, away from my loved ones and my familiar environment. Doubt crept in, but the excitement of the adventure set in, and we were off. I consumed everything.

On the train, we received frequent visits from our tour guide, Dinshaw, from the Lalla Tour Company, which we were travelling with. He was an attractive and charming young man. He sang English songs every night and taught them to us. We all joined him in a chorus. I still remember that Amta and I learned to sing Pat Boone's song

> *"A Mocking Bird on the willow Tree, Looking for lovers below.........*

Amta and I were young friends on our first adventure. We would giggle as we sang this song over and over again. The epitome was when we heard the line of this Pat Boone's song:

> *"Now the moral is this, if you want to kiss..............*
> we were hysterical.

It tickled us because neither of us had a boyfriend, nor had we kissed anyone before. Fifty five years ago, in India, dating was unheard of, and we were only budding teenagers. So we daydreamed about the "Loving Prince" whom we would kiss someday. Amta and I bonded on this trip tremendously. We developed a friendship that has lasted for a lifetime.

The first stop on our trip was *New Delhi*. Our group was driven around the city to see the famous monuments. We saw the Red Fort, which is built with red sand stones, the India Gate, and Humayun's tomb. We also visited Raj Ghat, which is a black marble platform that marks the spot where Mahatma Gandhi, the father of India, was cremated. At Raj Ghat, there is an eternal flame left open to the sky. It was a peaceful place that caused me to learn as much as I can about Gandhi's life.

After visiting New Delhi, we drove to *Agra*, the location of one of the Wonders of the World: the Taj Mahal. The Taj Mahal was built by the Mughal emperor, Shah Jahan, in loving memory of his wife, Mumtaz Mahal. I had read about it but had never imagined its exquisite beauty and size. The monument is built with white marble inlaid with precious stones. I was in a state of awe. I learned a bit of Mughal history as we visited buildings like the Taj Mahal, but I could not get the loving prince, the eternal flame and white marble out of my head.

From Agra, we started off to our final destination, *Kashmir*, which remains the most beautiful and scenic place I have ever visited, even to this day. We stayed in a houseboat surrounded by spectacular natural beauty. Every morning, the local people would come in their boats with fresh, homegrown fruits. I had never eaten such juicy strawberries, raspberries and cherries. Flowers bloomed everywhere. There was a vitality that consumed me.

Amta and I overindulged on cherries, and the next day, Amta had an upset stomach. She felt so bad that she could not go on the group sightseeing tour. I told the teacher that I would stay back with her. Amta was very touched by my gesture. The group went on the tour, and we sat and talked and laughed all day long while Amta recovered from her overindulgence. We learned a lot about each other, our aspirations, and our families. We grew closer.

During this trip, I loved to pose for and take pictures. Amta took pictures of me in the new camera that Dadaji had given me. I have saved one of my favorite pictures from this trip – of me in a Kashmiri outfit – for over sixty years. It really stuck, an image capturing not just the adventure, but the internal struggle. I took many pictures of the Himalayan landscape with my new camera. The film couldn't be developed until I returned to Mumbai, so I had no idea how the pictures would come out. At every step, I felt very grateful to Dadaji for giving me this camera and sending me on this trip. I owed him my gratitude. He gave me this experience, the freedom.

Our trip ended and we returned home with memories, pictures and experiences of a lifetime. After I returned back home, the pictures were developed. Most of these pictures came out well. I developed confidence in my photography, which eventually became one of my passions. Dadaji was visibly happy. He had allowed me, a granddaughter, to travel without family – a very unusual thing for a parent or grandparent to do in those days. He commented that I had matured on this trip.

With a smirk on his face, he said, "Someday, I want to send you abroad."

The seeds of my travel dreams were already planted. In my culture, people did not typically express love, verbally or physically, towards an older person or a person of the opposite gender. I expressed my gratitude to Dadaji through my eyes, which were overflowing with tears of joy.

My trip to Kashmir helped to foster two of the most important relationships of my life. Dadaji had made it possible for me to travel, and we became emotionally closer after this trip. The trip had also enabled me to develop a lifelong bond with my friend Amta. These two played a role in my emotional development, parenting, and self.

As Amta and I grew up, got married, and had children, we remained friends. I moved to the United States in 1970, and Amta continued living in India. Two continents, one friendship! This friendship, though, was not shaken by the long distance between us and the slow means of communication. We are the type of best friends that do not need to see each other all the time, talk every day, but when we do talk, the world stops and we pick up where we left off. Amta visited me in America three times during the forty-eight years I have lived here, and I visited India numerous times. Many of these trips were with our children. Our husbands liked each other, and our children began to bond. On each of my trips back to India, I reserved one day to spend with Amta, and each time, we just talked and caught up on what had happened since my previous visit. We compared notes on our married life, our jobs, and the challenges of raising children. Invariably, we reflected upon our first trip to Kashmir together. It all goes back to Kashmir.

In 2013, Amta and her husband, Hatim, visited us at my request, so that Hatim could also visit the beautiful, places in America. We drove them to Niagara Falls. My husband, Viren, and Hatim started to talk at a deeper level, which surprised Amta and me. Before it had only been cordial, polite, not phony but distant. Amta smiled. On our return, we all felt the comfort to plan a longer trip together, just the four of us – this time in India. All five of our children were very happy that we were planning this trip. For Amta and I, this would be the first time since our high school trip to Kashmir that we would be able to enjoy traveling together. We were two girls again.

Over fifty years after we first travelled together, we planned a trip together to *Amritsar, Delhousie, Dharamshala,* and *Chandigarh,* in North India. Circumstances were different this time, though. We were traveling with our husbands, and we were not the giggly free birds we were on our first trip. Throughout our trip, Amta took pictures of me and Viren, and we took pictures of Amta and Hatim. It felt like Deja vu: taking each other's photos on vacation just as we had done over fifty years earlier, but this time with our iPhones. A lot changed, nothing changed in our hearts.

Amta had chosen the tour company and made the itinerary. We flew from Mumbai to Amritsar. For the remainder of our trip, we travelled by car with a driver, and the driver was also our tour guide. We were fascinated by the history lesson that our tour guide gave us as we travelled through the state of Punjab. Punjab is the land of five rivers: Ravi, Sutlej, Chenab, Beas and Jhelum. The ancient Punjab is the land of the Vedas, Indus Valley civilization, and Taxila University (an ancient University in India). It was fulfilling to travel through a land where the earliest civilizations of *Mohenjo Daro* and *Harappa* had developed. Something like I would later experience in *Jerusalem*. Places that civilization has grown out of can never move beyond this, but they are paralyzed in a beauty that ceases to stop, relentlessly finding its way through old streets, fishermen, the homeless children. These places know something we do not.

Amritsar, located in the state of Punjab, is well known for its Golden Temple, a sacred place for the Sikhs, and is an incredible place for tourists to visit, it is quite literally a temple made out of gold. I was speechless as I watched the temple volunteers feed thousands of people who visited that day. They do this every day for free and as part of their spiritual responsibility. We visited the temple during the day and at night, and each visit was moving in its own unique way. The Golden Temple is surrounded by water, and the reflection is incomparable. The sights and the sounds of the Golden Temple captured my mind and soul. I did not want to leave that place.

After visiting the Golden Temple, we learned about other aspects of Amritsar's rich history. It is the birthplace of Luv and Kush (Sons of Rama and Sita, from the Epic Ramayana). Amritsar also borders with Pakistan. Every evening on the border, called Wagah Border, the Indian and Pakistani armies conduct a ceremony when the gate at the border is opened. During the preceding hour, the soldiers march to the music and sing patriotic songs. I was proud of the country I was born in. I was proud of our armed forces. I was simply proud.

After watching the Wagah Border ceremony, we all talked about the partition between India and Pakistan, which split families, which is a terrible thing. Amta and Hatim are Muslim and have cousins in Pakistan. Some of their uncles had chosen to move to Pakistan at the time of partition, while Amta's and Hatim's parents chose to stay in India. Although Viren and I are Hindus and Amta and Hatim are Muslims, we could openly talk about the history of animosity between our two religions. These were emotional conversations for all of us. They always were based on respect, something that would not hurt the American psyche.

On the next day, we drove for almost six hours to *Dalhousie*. We could see the grandeur of the Himalayas at every turn on our drive, ominously staring us down, reminding us of their omnipotence, their fury, their wisdom and age. Dalhousie is a paradise and a tourist's dream. It is located in Himachal Pradesh, which is one of the most beautiful states in India, where landscaping knows no bounds, and the only boundaries are the giants above, unless you take on that challenge.

Our hotel was located on a hill. Our rooms were connected by adjoining balconies, which faced the mighty snowcapped Himalayas. The mountains looked different at dawn and dusk, an explosion of light and the shadow, but we were always in their shadow. The Himalayas have a way of looking at you. If you are not a religious person, after seeing them you believe in something, you are compelled to. Amta and I called out for each other every time we saw a monkey jump from a tree to our balcony. I never wanted to leave. It was a place I sunk deeper to, where I enjoyed things such as a breath of air, a cloud, my best friend and my husband.

After staying in Dalhousie for two days, we headed to *Dharamshala*. This *hill station* is home to the Tibetan Buddhist monk, the Dalai Lama. Though I fantasized that we might be able to meet him, none of his disciples knew where he was traveling at that time. The Tibetan Monastery was very beautiful, especially the huge statue of sitting Buddha. Visiting the statue of Buddha was a peaceful and spiritual experience.

Tourists were not allowed to take photos from the room in which the Buddha sat. Amta and I lay down on the floor of the surrounding balcony to capture a photo of the magnanimous sitting Buddha. But, it was hard for us to get up again. Unlike during our high school trip to Kashmir, now we were in our seventies and suffering from osteoarthritis. Amta and I laughed at our growing age-related limitations. We both were reminded of our continuous giggling as teenagers during our first trip together. It was quite a sight. We always share something.

In the late evenings in Dharamshala, our husbands went to bed early while Amta and I continued to visit shops with Tibetan handicrafts. We learned about the Tibetan people who had emigrated from Tibet to India after the India-China war.

Our final destination on the trip was *Chandigarh*. This is the most well-planned and modern city that I have ever visited in India. We learned that it had been planned by a famous French architect. We visited Asia's largest rose garden, spread over thirty acres of land. It has sixteen-hundred different species of roses in every color you could possibly imagine. Amta and I could not stop taking pictures of these colorful roses, like children again.

We also visited *Nek Chand*'s unique, world-acclaimed rock garden. It is an amazing masterpiece, created in the form of an open-air garden. The entire place has sculptures made out of rocks of various sizes and exquisite artwork made from different waste materials like broken glass. The stories we heard about its owner, *Nek Chand*, were very inspiring. His family had to move to a village, now part of Chandigarh, after the British left the divided countries of India and Pakistan. He started the garden secretly in his spare time. He spent over twenty years personally creating more than two-thousand sculptures using stones, debris, and other discarded junk that was left over from the fifty plus villages that were destroyed in order to build the modern city of Chandigarh. The garden is an epitome of creativity and innovation, of rebirth after destruction. I was visibly sad when Amta recently shared the news of Nek Chand's passing at ninety years of age. Amta and I talked about the emotional connection we have to places that we have visited, as opposed to those we have just learned about in books, and when you see something, if you are paying attention, you really see it.

As our tour came to an end and we returned home with tons of pictures and more importantly memories of a lifetime. And as we had hoped, Amta and I were able to relive the special bonding that had begun during our first trip to Kashmir. Both trips that Amta and I took together epitomized the qualities of traveling that have inspired me to continue to seek out new travel adventures throughout my life. Between our first and this one, a lot of things changed. I had to take a break from traveling, pursue education, raise a family and grow up. As I've come to believe—and see—we have many chapters in our lives. Some we are aware of, many aware still. Medical school was a chapter that had closed and led to the beginning of another. This is when I began to travel, see the world, and become what I am becoming.

Nalini's wanderlust had just begun, India

Nalini in Kashmir, the dream land, India

From Left, Hatim, Amta, Nalini, Viren at the Golden Temple, India

Golden Temple, Amritsar, India

Nalini in Nek Chand's world acclaimed

Out of the country: My Eyes Were on the World

The final medical exams were over; I just graduated from medical school and obtained a Medical degree, MBBS. It was time to relax, time to do anything but study. I wanted to plan a trip to get away, a refocusing. My annual trip with my grandmother, where we visit relatives in *Rajkot, Gujarat*, was long overdue. It sounded perfect.

During that visit, while I was fully engrossed in having fun with my cousins, I received a letter from my friend Prafulla, stating that other classmates of mine were studying for an exam given by Educational Council for Graduate Medical Education *(ECFMG)*. Now, I had already registered to take the exam but did not start any preparation. I was behind. This worried me because the only way to pursue higher education in the United States was to pass this exam. Anyone with a medical degree from outside the United States who wants to specialize in a medical specialty needs to pass this exam. There was a problem though: this exam was not given in India. This exam was proctored in Ceylon which is now renamed as *Sri Lanka*. Students traveled from far away to take this exam.

I knew my ambition was to get a postgraduate education in the United States. It was this ambition, wanting to be a practicing doctor *in America* that made me board my first international flight. A beginning of sorts, but really a first step out into the world, outside of India, and into my future.

The male members of my family were concerned that as a female it was outrageous of me to plan to go abroad, alone. Obviously, to travel abroad you need a passport, and I did not have one. When I brought the idea of applying for a passport to my family, these family members did not want me to go to passport office by myself. They feared that if I had a passport it would open up many doors for me to travel abroad. They wanted me to stay close, stay local, and not leave them. In their opinion, it was not right for me to do. In my community there were very few people who had college education. In fact, most elders believed that women should learn household activities, get married and establish a family. Not become a doctor, and especially not become a doctor in the United States. Although they did know I overcame stereotypical thinking and prejudices to become a doctor, they still held onto the past tradition. The one I was stepping out of. I aspired to do things that were frowned upon by my elders. They were tradition bound. They meant well, they really did. But I had a free spirit that could not be confined within the norms of the society. I was a child born into the confinements of tradition bound India, but I wanted more, my wants were different.

I applied for my passport by myself without anyone accompanying me. This was an unusual and unacceptable step in the culture in which I was growing up. I received my passport! I felt like I had a license to travel. My maternal grandmother, "Ma" as I addressed her, was proud of me. She trusted my judgment. She trusted my instinct to leave, to do what many people do not. She was proud that I had the strength to fight not only against tradition and prejudice, but my own family. Sure, it may be strength, but I call it adventure. And this first adventure out of the country was about to begin.

My medical school classmate, Madhuri and I set out to travel together. We both had never sat on an airplane, let alone leave the country. I did not even have money to buy my airline tickets. This could have been problematic, obviously, but I used my resources. I needed to get to Sri Lanka. I approached my Dadaji, who had always supported my decisions: a man who always had faith in me, a man that navigated between tradition and my free spirit. He was also apprehensive about the ten thousand mile journey to the United States that would follow this trip to take the exam. I would travel, ten thousand miles away from home; alone, without a family member accompanying me. My eyes were not set on Sri Lanka, they were set on the United States, the stars and stripes, the land of the free, and for me—the land of the unknown. He bought the airline tickets for me. I knew I had his blessings, and even though no women in my family traveled abroad alone, he knew I could, and would regardless of his generous support. I would find a way.

When the reality of travelling abroad set in, I began to think about actual details of this life changing experience. In essence, I had to plan everything. I had to figure out where to stay, where to eat, where to study. I arranged to stay in a student hostel in Colombo, Sri Lanka. One problem solved. But there came a bigger one. I ate only vegetarian food, and I did not have any idea as to the availability of vegetarian food in places I was traveling. Those days our informants were people who had travelled before us, not smartphones, not Google, certainly not Siri. I did read travel books however but they did not provide information about vegetarian food availability, it was simply not on the map. Although, outwardly I looked calm and stayed in control, my inner self was fearful and insecure. My comfort zone was ripped, shredded, torn apart. I really was on my own, outside of my box.

Finally, the day of our departure arrived. My family escorted me to the airport. I was tearful as I bid goodbye to everyone. This time, my school friends and adult teachers were not accompanying me. It was just me and my one friend. We alone on our adventure to Sri Lanka, although deep down inside I knew my trip will go well beyond that island.

As the flight took off, my excitement grew. Madhuri and I sat next to an older gentleman on the plane. He was a businessman; had no children and he had travelled to Colombo many times in the past. He did not share any other information about himself with us although we told him all about us. We started to address him as "*Uncle*" a traditional respectful address. I asked him all kinds of questions about Colombo, its people, means of transportation to the site where exam was given and about availability of vegetarian food. I could not help but ask this because I was worried. We began to tell him more about us, about what we were setting out to do, about what we were taking on. He became interested in our venture and provided us information about this new land. He was very familiar with Indian culture and looked somewhat perplexed that two young women were traveling by themselves to take an examination. Needless to say, he had sensed our anxiety about our new venture. With this sense of anxiety, he helped point us in the right direction.

We arrived in *Sri Lanka*. It was like a second paradise. We were not sure about transportation, but Uncle rented a car and offered to drive us to our destination. We accepted with gratitude. The hostel was the least expensive boarding we could find, so it made sense. We made it work. As our car rolled along the beach side roads, I was shocked to see the turquoise blue ocean water and the white sandy beaches. I had never seen the water so clean and this color fascinated me. I did not even know water could be this color and that trees could sway peacefully next to the ocean and the white beach. A piece of machinery, an airplane, was the bridge between my home and the piercing blue and white ocean and the beach. We arrived at our destination, still remembering we were there to take an exam. We thought that we were now alone, facing the rest of our challenges by ourselves. No more Uncle! The transportation and lodging was done, but we still needed to figure out the other things, like food. While bidding goodbye, the kind gentleman offered to accompany us to the examination site on the next day. Our faces turned red as smiles spread all over them. We accepted his offer and felt relaxed. We were speechless and did not really know how to thank him. He truly had saved us not only money, but confusion and anxiety, he made our first adventure simple, easy, all with kindness.

The next day we took the exam. We had no idea what the outcome would be, but for the time, we were relaxed. After the exam we had one additional day to spend in Colombo. Uncle took us sightseeing. We found vegetarian food in small joints operated by Indians who had immigrated to Sri Lanka decades ago. Familiar faces in an unfamiliar place! Although we spent some significant time together with our new friend "Uncle", he hardly told us anything about his personal life. However, he looked happy to watch us excited in this new land. But the questions did not need to be asked, he gave of himself, his resources, his heart. We graciously accepted his help, his experience. He was the guide we never set out for, the guide we would need.

It was an amazing experience because I learned to communicate with strangers. In this new land, Uncle showed us around and helped us, total strangers. I was impressed that the world had so many good people who selflessly take interest in others and reach out to help them. I lost my fear of strangers; a fear that was instilled in me by my family because they wanted me to be safe. But I was safe, I was out of my box, I did what they told me not to, and loved it.

After spending three days in Colombo, Sri Lanka, I returned back home; more confident and self-assured, more traveled. The customs officer at Mumbai airport started to interrogate me about things I had purchased in Sri Lanka, especially drugs. I was unaware that young people brought in drugs from Sri Lanka.

Since I said that I did not have anything beyond my personal belongings on me, he was surprised and wanted to know more about the purpose of my travels. I felt the comfort to answer all his questions. I realized that communicating the truth to anyone was easy and made me feel comfortable. I had nothing to hide. The interrogation made me feel uncomfortable to start but then I realized I had nothing to be afraid of as I had done nothing wrong. My confidence was high, higher than a hotel view of the setting sun we watched in Colombo at the beach after the exam.

After returning back home, I told our stories to my family, especially about the kind gentleman who had become our Uncle in the true sense. My family wanted to meet him and offer their gratitude as well. This Uncle was the connection between their fear and my success. He helped make my first international trip pleasurable and he helped build my confidence in my travel capabilities. I contacted our new guardian to introduce him to my family members since he was also expected to return back to Mumbai in a week. But, he was not reachable.

Colombo was the last time I ever saw him. He came in the breeze over the turquoise water that floated above the sand. He came and showed us around, helped us adjust, offered himself, and simply vanished from my life. He wanted nothing in return. I think he just wanted to help, and that he did. To this date, I think about this gentleman as a saintly man who came and left my life after having made a difference. But there were many differences in my world now. My horizon was expanding. I began to think that there are people in this universe who have a purpose in life. They make a difference in the life of others and move on. He just moved on, like the breeze, He inspired me to be like him, willing to reach out to others without any expectations.

My maternal grandfather, whom I addressed as *"Bapaji,"* was totally surprised. Having ventured on my own I had learned to become more expressive and assertive, more confident. I had also learned to ask for help when I needed someone to guide me. I had become thoughtful and self-assured. I could stand on my own two feet, travel, eat, make it by, succeed and excel. They were developing faith in me.

I realized that through travels my interest in communicating with people had expanded. I liked conversation; I liked hearing about other people's lives. I had come out of a sheltered life and learned how to meet my needs and find vegetarian food. Although this food was not the same as I was traditionally used to, I enjoyed the culinary habits of people in other cultures. This was a huge relief to me because I did not want to compromise on my values, especially to continue to be a vegetarian. I did not compromise my food habits. I adjusted my comforts to the challenges presented in front of me. I impressed my family along the way. I had confidence, they had confidence, but I wanted more. I knew that this want was far beyond Sri Lanka. So I pursued that. I knew I could do it, but it required courage to break tradition. I broke out of my comfort zone, and broke into the world of travel. It did not stop there, and I do not think it ever will. Chapter after chapter, travel remained constant.

I wanted to visit Sri Lanka as a tourist, under different circumstances. I had learned about the characters of the great epic Ramayana as a child. The war between good and evil had occurred in Lanka which was named Ceylon by the British and currently known as Sri Lanka.

That time arrived. This was my second visit to Sri Lanka. There was no comparison as the first one was 50 years ago when I was a novice traveler who had stepped out of my home country India to take an exam. Success in this exam was to take me to the US and open up doors to the world from inside as well as outside. A beautiful life journey indeed! It was like making almost a full circle around the world and back to Sri Lanka from where my international tours had begun.

We were now tourists. We had more resources to explore the country. We chose to spend less time in Colombo, a large and growing city with upcoming tall towers. I enjoy being in bustling cities but my impression from all the travels has been that the real culture can be witnessed in the interior small towns and villages by talking with the locals, listening to their life experiences, eating with them and sharing stories.

Sri Lanka offers beautiful white sandy beaches on its south east coast, mountains with tea gardens, lush greenery, spice gardens and botanical gardens. These towns had other significance to our Hindu culture. The epic *Ramayana* that depicts the war between good (Rama) and evil (Ravana) occurs partly in India and partly in Sri Lanka. I remembered many stories I had heard in childhood about Rama and Ravana (*the good and the evil*). It was a nostalgic feeling to be standing on places where this great epic had begun and ended.

Ravana the mighty king of Sri Lanka 8000 years ago was a great decipher of Lord Shiva. After having received all the power, he became power maniac and wanted to defeat Rama from India. He kidnaped *Rama's wife, Sita,* and brought her to Sri Lanka to make her his favorite queen. Although Sita turned him down, Ravana captivated her in the mountains, a place called *Ashoka Vatica.* All these places have been preserved and the faithful Hindus have made a *Sita Temple* preserved Ravana's palace and named waterfalls after his name. One major character in this epic Ramayana is *Hanuman*, a powerful loyal disciple of Rama. He was given the task to find Sita.

The team of monkeys under the leadership of Hanuman created a bridge between southern tip of India and Sri Lanka. This bridge known as *Setu Bridge* has sunk under water today but NASA has provided pictures taken from the space showing its existence under water.

The Hindu believers of Sri Lanka has built a Hanuman temple

and created statues of Sita and Hanuman where Hanuman finds her and convinces her that Rama had sent her a ring which would help her recognize Hanuman as his envoy. The story continues that Rama fights a war with Ravana, rescues Sita and leaves Sri Lanka after giving the kingdom to Ravana's brother *Vibhishana*. The palace of Vibhishana is also preserved however part of it has become a Buddhist temple built when Buddha visited Sri Lanka for the third time.

The population of Sri Lanka is 70% Buddhist, 30% Hindus, Christians and Muslims. Some Hindu temples and Buddhist temples co-exist in Colombo. I could not cease to admire the architecture, paintings and statues of Buddha no matter how many times I visit these temples. Although a Hindu by birth, I am not a ritualistic worshipper in actions. I do however; believe in the philosophy of the religions.

The towns called *Kandy* and *Neuvaria Elia* have preserved the history and culture of the country which was considered highly prosperous for its resources; tea gardens, spices, coconuts, sapphire, moon stones and other precious stones. Sri Lanka was known as the golden country. The Dutch, followed by the Portuguese and Britain were attracted to these resources. British ruled the country until 1948. Subsequently, there was an internal war between the Tamil Tigers and local government which ended five years ago. The stories about this war are similar to the ones going on between Palestine and Israel.

Sri Lanka also has several national parks where Asian elephants and leopard attract the tourists to go on safari. We were enchanted by an elephant orphanage called *Pinnawala* where the orphan baby elephants are raised. They are fed milk in bottles, taken to the river for bath. The creative natives take elephant poo and process it using several steps, which we watched. The final product is paper from which paper products are made. This "Poo Paper" is the most creative product.

There are two mountain peaks, Adam's peak which is believed to have footprints of Buddha according to Buddhists, and Adam's footprints according to the Christians. The second one Sigriya Mountain where tourists climb 3000 steps to look at the remains of ancient palace and gardens

We did not climb these steps for health reasons. Many of these places do not have medical facilities or equipment if a medical emergency arises. Dambulla caves where sleeping Buddha and in several postures have been preserved. There is a beautiful temple where Buddha's relic tooth has been preserved. Each one of these sightseeing places has exciting things to offer that inspired us every step of our journey

Ma, Amta, Kantimama, Padmamami, Batuben, Kalpesh,
Manjeri, amongst many who came to Mumbai airport
to fare goodbye to Viren and Nalini, India

Arriving in America

A lthough I was not born in America, it has become my base, my nest, my Home. It is where we raised our family. My husband, Viren, and I dated for a few weeks. We had similar aspirations to pursue our postgraduate medical studies abroad and travel all over the world. This was an immediate connection. We got married by traditional arranged marriage on May 31, 1970.

Viren had completed his postgraduate studies and received his board certification leading to MD degree in Cardiology in India. I had completed my MBBS (Medical Degree). Viren had applied for a job in the United States and received an internship position in Highland Park, Michigan. I had yet to pass the qualifying exam—which I would soon—to start an internship in the States, but we were excited to travel abroad to a new land ten thousand miles away from home. We had no other support but we had each other, and it felt like we were on our honeymoon since we were married for only a month. As time came close to starting our long journey, I was filled with mixed emotions. I had known my husband for three months, one of which we were actually married. I was about to leave my familiar environment, my family and friends to charter a new territory. My entire family including my grandparents, my mother and my sister, my uncle, aunts and two cousins, Viren's parents and his sister, brothers, and their wives had all come to the airport to bid us farewell. My best friend Amta was there at the airport too. If you couldn't already tell, we were tied by an arranged marriage, where two families had become one large family.

Unlike other travels this one was very different. We had borrowed money to buy our airline tickets. We had no idea if and when we will return back home and see all our loved ones again. But we had each other to start a new life in a new land. Together alone, we journeyed into the unknown, with nothing aside from medical degrees, vegetarian diets, and newly found love and companionship. I had a travel mate. I was leaving a "Home" not knowing when I will return back.

En route to Highland Park, Michigan, we took lay overs in three places—Athens, Paris and London—to do some sightseeing. I had expected that my experiences in the western world will be different, but Paris was, extraordinary. It was more than the books could describe, more than the pictures I saw. You can see from pictures, but you cannot smell, and you cannot feel. The French did not understand the English that we spoke; I suppose it was heavily accented. One incident is stuck in my mind permanently. We were one of the three couples in a restaurant for dinner. We managed to explain to the waiter that we were vegetarians and in those days we had to explain that vegetarian meant no fish, no meat, no chicken, and no pork. The waiter made a confused face and said, "Then what do you eat?" He gave us the menu and we requested glasses of water while we could figure out what we can order. Once again he gave us a look, which conveyed to us that he was thinking we had descended from another planet, something beneath the French culinary appetite. He seemed not to understand what kind of a drink was water. We all tried to explain in different tones of voices and with different accents but to no avail. Then all of a sudden Viren said "Aqua..Aqua..." A smile came over his face and he ran inside the kitchen yelling out loud "Aqua...Aqua...Aqua". In few minutes he brought us a wine bottle filled with water. We all started to drink water, glass after glass. It was summer and we were used to drinking water. None of us had tried alcoholic drinks in our lives.

Then an entourage of people came out from the kitchen and surrounded our round table, clapping and laughing as we drank water and satisfaction covered our faces. My opinion changed, these people were happy to have someone different in their graces.

We ordered toast and salad as those were the only items we knew we could safely eat as vegetarians. My cultural lessons about food had just begun, and as food is the gateway to a culture, my cultural lessons had just begun, too.

Our next stop was London. Among the many things that come to mind, the most notable was to see bright daylight until ten o'clock at night. Days were longer in summer. We could do more things, see more places. Life seemed longer in the summer. I learned about the weather and seasonal changes in the western parts of the world that I had never experienced in India. We had rainy season, hot summers and very mild winters in Mumbai. The weather in London blew my mind. I hadn't experienced Michigan yet. That was, as they say, eye opening.

After arriving in Highland Park, Michigan, our biggest challenge was that we had very little money. Our apartment was assigned to us by my husband's employer, a local hospital. We had no choice but to live there. Although in India we emerged from a middle class family, we had more amenities than what we were given in this apartment. We realized that in this new land we were not only poor immigrants, but also very poor doctors, something we did not think that would happen.

My husband started his internship on July 1, 1970. He worked overnight for straight 36 hours when he was on call, which was every third night, and when he got home he could barely keep his eyes open, leave aside listening to my stories about what I had to go through to find us food. We had no car and in the suburbs of Michigan, there was hardly any public transportation.

I realized that to survive in this new land I had to make the most of what were my strengths. Although I felt I was all alone, I spoke English and I communicated with total strangers with ease and with a smile, the smile is important. To my surprise these strangers responded and tried to help me to the best of their abilities. I walked to supermarkets every day—half an hour each way—and brought home food that I could both afford and carry. I was surprised that when I crossed the streets the cars stopped and allowed me to walk through. There was hardly any one walking on the streets, so I figured this was a gesture to show courtesy.

My husband received his first paycheck after two weeks. We had very little money on us, so this was exciting and important. Our apartment did not have bed sheets, pillowcases, pots and pans. Some of these necessities were not available in supermarkets. I went to ask the superintendent of our building, whether there were any other stores I could walk to and buy these necessities. He was astonished but showed compassion as I explained my situation. He said that he and his wife visit a K-Mart every week by car, and proceeded to invite me to join them and buy what I needed. I was hopeful and felt touched by another person's kindness. The beginning in America was bleak, but we slowly started to pave the way with some help.

I remember thinking how important it will be to budget my husband's first paycheck. Well, that day came and he turned it over to me, which I quickly cashed and accepted the superintendent's offer to join him and his wife to go shopping. I bought an iron—the most expensive item—since my husband would need to wear a clean and well-ironed white coat every day. Next item was a small fan. Our apartment had one small window and there was no ventilation. I bought one bed sheet, one pillowcase, one pot, two dishes and two sets of silverware. All these items were adequate to get started. We didn't need much.

We were very happy even with limited means. I never

complained to my husband, instead took all these challenges in a stride. We wrote letters to families and friends in India. I wrote rosy exciting stories in the letters about the place where we lived and how happy we were. In those days, letters took almost a month to reach India; so every other month we exchanged letters. It was a slow, although rewarding process of communication. Each letter brought another world with it and the anticipation simply exacerbated this.

We began to accommodate to the new land, new working conditions and a new culture. Although Viren was working hard learning new ways of dealing with patients and new technologies, his clinical skills were sharper than most of his superiors. I decided to learn about the new culture while adapting to the new environment while I was waiting on starting my medical career. I must say that these challenges began to become exciting as I overcame them one by one. I was also enjoying the process of learning new things every day. I was a blank slate then, and it was in these first few months that I solidified my interest new challenges and new beginnings—new chapters.

At the end of two months we saved down payment to buy a brand new car on installments. None of us had driven a car in India. This excited us beyond belief; we were going to be able to drive ourselves around. Viren worked most of the time so I used the car to drive to places. People in this wonderful land taught me about parking meters, and gave me some driving tips. I began to make new friends. I was more mobile and accessible. I did not need to join the superintendent and his wife anymore; I could go on my own.

My very first friend in Michigan was Cora, an African American nurse who had a master's degree in English. She worked in the same hospital where Viren worked. She spoke eloquently. She reached out and taught me about the "Racial issues" and that in America the color of the skin actually mattered. In India, I knew that people were light skinned or dark skinned brown, but both brown. I must say that people preferred to have light skin, especially women, though. She was highly protective of me as she saw that I was quite naïve and people would take advantage of me. Perhaps she liked my veil of consciousness, my outsider view of not only color, but Americanism.

One day Viren and I met a middle-aged man in a department store. He was clearly not a Caucasian and not an African-American. He looked somewhat like us, with brown skin, black hair, and brown eyes. He walked straight towards us and yelled out loud. "My country man, you are here!"

We were amazed to see his reaction and felt kind of good. It was like meeting a long lost friend although we had never met him, a familiar face. He told us that he worked for Chrysler automobile company in Detroit and he had lived in America since age eighteen. He had arrived here on a ship from Eastern part of India, which is now Bangladesh. He introduced us to his Italian wife. He insisted on meeting us every weekend, and we accepted his offer whenever Viren was not on call on the weekend. He and his wife would arrive early in the morning and take us around on a tour of some sightseeing places. A friendship developed and we began to get closer. One day he took us to his house. We learned that it was his American dream to live in a house, his own house. Although he was not a vegetarian, he understood our dietary needs and was accommodating. He had not returned back to his homeland ever since he had jumped from the ship to start a new life in America, he never looked back. Through all his kind gestures it was palpable that he missed "his motherland, his people," as he would frequently say. We somehow fulfilled the craving for his motherland for him. He didn't need to go back. We gave him what he needed, I suppose, but then again maybe he just preferred it here. I wondered if he ever faced racially biased attitude, experienced the hate that Cora would warn us about.

I did not experience the discrimination Cora had described for me. I considered that people who do not know me are bound to be skeptical about me. I took it upon myself to talk to them about my culture and my place of origin. I was very surprised that people in America took keen interest in learning and understanding my culture, I thought they would be too much into themselves. It was from then on that I developed a notion that people who are not familiar with cultures and ways of life of other people tend to be skeptical of those who are different, which is then perceived as discrimination. Skepticism or not, I never really felt marginalized, maybe I was blinded to it beneath my veil, or maybe I simply encountered open minded people. America is a big place, not everywhere is filled with bigots, and not every place is filled with open-minded people. Maybe I was just lucky. Regardless of that, I took it upon myself to help those people understand my culture and I learned from them about their culture, a cultural exchange that fostered and developed into mutual respect. I enjoyed making new friends from all walks of life and learning about their cultures. It is the only way to grow as a person. Mark Twain was right when he said, "Travel is fatal to prejudice, bigotry, and narrow-mindedness, and many of our people need it sorely on these accounts. Broad, wholesome, charitable views of men and things cannot be acquired by vegetating in one little corner of the earth all one's lifetime." I was trying to be ahead of the curve, as so many immigrants are. You know there is something else aside from the little slice of paradise you inhabit, the little bit of land where you dwell. You die knowing you came so far and have seen more than the man who never leaves. They might be happy, but awakened, or perhaps they may be asleep. I was trying to stay awake. Was I "Home?" This emotional turmoil of being at "Home" was on my mind.

First Trip to Canada, the Land Above

Fast forward a year. It was April 1971 and Viren had signed a contract to continue his training in Internal Medicine and Cardiology in New York, starting July 1, 1971. He had two weeks of vacation to take before moving on to New York. By this time we had purchased a car, and a TV—the pots and pans and iron were old news. We had paid our debt and saved $1,000. A move to NY was ahead of us and we had no idea about the expenses we would encounter for housing in NY. Of course, they were enormous. But that was down the line.

We debated whether to vacation or stay home and rest during those two weeks and I was a bit tired. I was reminded that one of our missions to come to the USA was to travel, it was so accessible here. Highland Park, Michigan was very close to the Canadian border. We thought this was a great opportunity for us to travel to Canada. Although our budget was very small, we decided to drive and stay in roadside motels we could manage. We had a car after all.

We became members of American Automobile Association (AAA). I requested tour guides and Trip Tix for Canada. I thought this was an incredible service. They planned everything out; only in America! In India I had never learned to study maps to travel, and though it was difficult, I enjoyed reading the detailed map of Canada and started to plan out the route we would take to visit Canada starting from Niagara Falls to Toronto, Montreal, Quebec, Ottawa, Sue Saint Marie and then cross the Mackinaw bridge to enter back into Michigan. I designed our own great loop. The next task was to make reservations at roadside motels at various sites. Each of these motels was AAA rated which were acceptable to us. We spent $8-$10 per night at these hotels. It was 1971 when the gasoline prices ranged from 19-25 cents per gallon. This was all possible to do within our budget. Inflation laughs in these numbers faces; it was incredible we could travel for this little.

I cooked some vegetarian food that we can bring along and which can last for two to three days. I expected that we will learn more about the food that we can eat as we travel for a couple of days, but I wanted to be sure we would have some things in case. Well, that was not so. We had not eaten in a restaurant in Highland Park or around the area. We came upon a restaurant that looked inviting, so we gave it a try. The menu had items listed, which were unfamiliar to us. Our breakfast included tea, orange juice and a toast and for lunch we usually had French fries. For dinner we had salad and bread. These scheduled meals started to get boring after a few days, we wanted variety, and there was none. We read the menu but most of the listed items we did not understand. I was too embarrassed to ask about the ingredients in each item, maybe for personal reasons, or maybe I did not want to seem *too foreign*. Ingredients were not listed those days and it seemed that most waiters were trained to take orders as written on the menu and deliver, without any variation. We quickly learned that the smaller the restaurant the better was our chances that someone would take time and interest to learn about our needs and show us which item was vegetarian. However, we were willing to sacrifice our dietary needs over saving time to visit new places. Our culinary adventure did not expand much, but we did continue to learn about different items on the menus. Food was not that important, hunger was and is containable and we had stuff to see. It kept us on the move.

The excitement of Niagara Falls was captivating. It was our dream to be at the falls from the time we left India. What surprised me the most was that the lady who checked us in the motel had not seen the Niagara Falls? The motel was ten miles away from the falls and she lived in the vicinity. However, she seemed less enthusiastic about visiting such a magnanimous natural beauty, and here we were traveling to such places without having many resources. Were they really asleep?

Toronto and Montreal as large metropolitan cities were similar to Mumbai in many respects. All the memories of home came gushing down and filled my heart with mixed emotions. I missed my first home, India. I missed the busyness of the city,

While making reservations from far away in Highland Park, I had no real idea as to where each of our Motels was located. We arrived in Quebec and the motel was located on a lake in the rural part of the city. The scenic beauty was exquisite, but we were hungry and tired after driving the long distance through the remote part of Quebec. The restaurant was empty and the waiter was very friendly. We looked different to him, probably because of skin color, maybe expressions, I am not sure. But we did look different. I started to explain to him about our dietary restrictions while he listened very intently. Since majority of the people in Quebec spoke French, I was surprised that he made efforts to understand my English which was really speaking *"INDLISH"*. He went in the kitchen and brought with him the English-speaking chef. He seemed to understand our needs and more so wanted to help by cooking things that were not on the menu. He asked us if we were in a hurry and we said we would wait as long as he needed us to if we could get a homemade vegetarian meal. At the end of an hour he brought out white beans spiced to our taste, French bread and salad. He was delighted to watch us eat to the last bite on our plate. He did show some disappointment that we did not drink alcoholic beverages, and at that moment we were reminded of our experience in Paris only about a year ago. We began to understand the western culture where alcoholic beverages were part of a meal every day for most people. The chef was quite generous and it left an impact on our lives.

We felt more secured that we will be able to survive with our food habits. These experiences helped us understand people of different cultures and their own habits. The most inspiring thing was that there is a human language that goes beyond any other language when two people care and want to understand each other. We learned that they had a strong desire to help!

This was a fascinating tour of Canada within one year of our arrival in the United States. After leaving India, within a year we had already set foot in five different countries; Athens in Greece, Paris in France, London in Great Britain, Michigan in the United States, and several cities in Canada. We had learned tremendously about people, different cultures, languages, and food habits. It was just the beginning of a wonderful journey ahead. I think of what *Michael Palin* said, *"Once the travel bug bites there is no known antidote, and I know that I shall be happily infected until the end of my life."* This trip to Canada is where I fostered my connection to traveling, anywhere, anytime. It became an addiction! I knew I will return back to this beautiful scenic country.

Canadian Rockies: Several years passed but our dream to visit Canada was very much alive. Our children had grown up and we were empty nesters. Traveling to places where natural beauty abounds was on our mind. I looked to the land above again in planning for our next travel. The towering rugged mountains, pristine forests and majestic glaciers, blue waters of Lake Louis summarize the natural beauty of the *Canadian Rockies*. We took off. Our train journey from *Vancouver to Jasper Park, Banff Springs and Lake Louis* was an incredible experience which cannot be described in words. I took tons of pictures on Lake Louis with its turquoise blue water. Words can hardly describe mountains and their—not only effect—but look, feel, vibe, anything, really. They are spiritual beings that demand full respect and worship just the way Native Americans did.

Canada has so much more to offer, we realized! We wished that the time to return back to Canada would come soon.

Polar Bear Excursion: We have always loved wild life. The behavior of wild life has intrigued me forever since I was young. In my search for another travel opportunity in Canada, I came across a brochure by *Tauck Travel Company* where *Polar Bear Excursion* was offered. It was an opportunity to watch polar bears in their own habitats. I grabbed this opportunity before global warming may make it difficult. However, the environment where we would have to go was located in *Churchill, Canada*, which is considered the Polar Bear capital of the world. We literally had to go into their home. The time of the year we would have to go was October and November when Polar Bears come in large numbers to the Hudson Bay waiting for the bay to freeze and then they would go on the ice looking for their favorite food, seals. I looked up what Churchill's weather was like and it seemed to vary between 30 degree to minus 4 degree Fahrenheit and we had to add the wind chill factor. I was excited to take this tour but apprehensive about its chilling weather conditions. Then there was a concern about finding vegetarian food as we always have to keep in mind that finding food could be a challenge. As I mulled over this dilemma I remembered a native Alaskan woman who we had met some twenty years ago. She had told me that there was nothing like bad weather, if there is appropriate clothing on the body to tolerate it. I discussed this dilemma with Viren and he being more courageous and adventurous than me, got excited to take this tour. It was a tour of six days and the cost was close to a thousand dollars a day. We signed up almost a year ahead of time. There was no guarantee what Mother Nature had in store for us to be able to watch Polar Bears. But this was a chance we had to take.

Towards the end of winter in New York, I started to shop for layers of clothing. We needed synthetic material for clothing which would allow the skin to breathe. One of our suitcases was needed just for warm layered clothing. As September rolled in, Viral, our son, who goes skiing, examined all the clothing we had collected and ordered boots, balaclava ski masks, woolen socks, good gloves and mittens; everything in two layers.

Viral and his wife, Rupa, gave us their ski pants, helmets and goggles that they use in skiing.

We were prepared to go.

Early morning we flew from New York to *Winnipeg, in Manitoba, Canada*. We were there by noon. Winnipeg used to be the third largest city in North America when transportation was mainly by the railroad. However, with the opening of the Panama Canal the role of the railroad curtailed. Currently it ranks the tenth largest city in Canada.

Winnipeg University has diverse student body that has brought diversity to the city. A stretch limo came to pick us up at the airport. The showering of luxuries by Tauck Travel Company had just begun. Our hotel was modern with all amenities and it was located at the fork where two rivers met. It was called the Inn at Forks. Our window overlooked newly opened museum of Human Rights, an interesting looking building with a statue of Mahatma Gandhi in the entrance. It was inspiring and a proud moment to see how one human being had an impact on the world. We saw his statue in South Africa at the site where he was thrown off the train because a brown skinned man was not accepted in the first class even when he could afford to buy the first class tickets. We had seen his statue in Chile, South America as a symbol of independence without violence. He was known worldwide for Human Rights movement he had started in South Africa in 1869 and continued the independence movement in India until its independence from the British in 1947.

We went to the Terminal Market to eat their well-known cinnamon buns. They had come out fresh from the oven. Manitoba is well known for cultivating wild rice which we ate and bought some to bring home. While there, we visited the legislative building. Its architecture from inside and outside is exquisite. We then proceeded to Manitoba museum which was kept open just for our group. It was arranged by Tauck Travel Company. We watched First Nations people perform a hula-hoop dance. The instructor of these dancers told us that he was proud of his culture and wanted to pass it on to the younger generation. He told us that this dancing had replaced his alcohol addiction. It had brought back his dignity and respect. Being a psychiatrist, I was intrigued how such a healthy way of living life can get people out of addictive and self-destructive behaviors.

We had our first dinner with our tour companions. We were 25 all together and our tour director, Rob White was a handsome young man, articulate and caring. Our table was the noisiest. One couple was from Connecticut, one was from Hawaii and one lady was from Ottawa, Canada in addition to two of us. We bonded quickly and then on we had dinners together for all six days. We also visited the Human Rights museum which had just opened that week. We were emotionally touched to see Mahatma Gandhi's statue in the entrance of the museum.

Next morning our tour company had a chartered plane for us where we flew to reach *Churchill, Manitoba*. I had not travelled by a chartered plane before in my life. There was no waiting on security lines and boarding was a breeze. In two hours we were in Churchill. Stepping out of the plane, the first thing we noticed was a major difference in weather. Everything looked white. There was light snow on the ground. Just 24 hours ago we had left beautiful foliage in NY and now in Churchill there were few random evergreen trees. Most of them had lost their branches on north-east side which looked interesting but weird. We learned that northwest wind had destroyed those branches. The locals take two such trees with leaves, put them together and make one Christmas tree. *Very smart and creative, I thought!*

We arrived at our cozy new place, Lazy Bear Lodge for three nights. It was a log cabin made from 1000 logs of wood. During lunch, Wally, the owner came to greet everyone at each table and told us that he built the log cabin himself. There was also a beautiful stone fireplace which he had built for the dining area. He was proud to tell us that the lodge closes down by end of November, when the Hudson Bay freezes, Polar Bears are gone hunting for the seals and long winter takes over. There are about a 1000 people who live in Churchill year round and Wally does maintenance work inside the cabins during the winter. His wife, Donna, a lovely woman, had taken care of our vegetarian food. We could not believe that we had options of eating fresh food. We had not expected to have variety of vegetarian food which was tasty and flavorful in Churchill.

Then came two most important days when we were scheduled to go out along the Hudson Bay to watch those hungry bears just waiting for the bay to freeze so they can start hunting for the seal. Polar bears, while beautiful, are dangerous and powerful. They are real bears. When they stand on their two feet, they are ten feet tall. They are the iconic symbol of a threatened Arctic. The local people who first came to this area are called Inuit. They call the polar bear, *"Nanuk: wise, powerful, almost a man."* We learned that global warming has melted sea ice on which polar bears survive. It is up to our generation to save polar bears for our grandchildren and great grandchildren. When seals are not available polar bears eat almost anything including vegetation, berries, geese and bird eggs.

We all arrived at the Hudson Bay and got into our Tundra

buggy or crawler. This was a tall vehicle with huge tires that can go through creeks two to three feet deep, on rocks and on ice. We felt invincible.

Someone spotted the first polar bear, a mom and a cub. They were close, along the road eating seaweeds. Everyone started to assemble near two windows with all kinds of cameras to capture photos of these beautiful bears. Although everything around us was white covered with snow, the bears had a distinctive yellowish white fur that can be spotted from a distance. However, these bears were close by. We camped out watching their every move. We were told to be quiet and not startle the bears. I was able to take their photographs even with my little iPhone camera. I even got some video clips, especially of the cub trying to get through the hole in the tires of our buggy. The mother bear walked away in all directions, always looking back to keep a watchful eye on her cub. The cub was full of curiosity. We saw them stand on two feet like a man, right near our buggy. I was close to the window, and there I saw the mamma bear looking straight through the window. We made eye contact! I was excited, but not scared because we were in a highly protective environment.

We learned that her cub was about a year old. Female polar bears mate during spring, come ashore in summer and don't feed again until the following February. This means that they go for eight months without feeding, during which time they give birth and nurse their new cubs. The cubs, usually two, weigh only about 2-3 pounds at birth but get to twenty to thirty pounds in just three months if they both survive. The gestation period is only about three months; cubs are usually born during December month. They are therefore called Christmas bears. Polar bear moms spend two and a half years teaching their cubs how to live and hunt in the Arctic. We saw one cub that kept on moving away from the mom and we were told he was about two years old and exploring his independence. Mom bear also seemed less concerned and allowed him to wander. And then before the end of the day, two bears, a mom and a cub crossed the road right in front of us.

On the next day we saw one huge big male polar bear sitting under the tree. It was a windy day and snow was coming down. We were told that in such weather even polar bears like to be lazy. He kept on raising his head from time to time but did not move.

When polar bears are spotted, there is an active communication going on between drivers of other tundra buggies and other vans. Most of the people in those vehicles are photographers with huge lenses jutting out of their camera. Although the locals advise the tourists to watch the polar bears from far, and do nothing to threaten them; we saw a few people come out of their vehicle to take photographs. A mom bear went straight to the van and tried to place her paw in the window. The driver quickly reacted and rolled up his window and turned on the ignition. This sound startled the bear and she walked away. Such are dangerous situations. Polar bears have walked in the town where residents keep their doors open for anyone who may need to run indoors when encountered by a polar bear in town.

When polar bear becomes dangerous or walks in the town, people are informed to call the polar bear restrainers who may sedate them. We also visited a polar bear jail where such bears are kept for thirty days and then released far away on to the sea ice. The town of Churchill has closed dumpsters, which were left open in the past. They attracted polar bears to wander in the town. But since their closure polar bears are not spotted frequently in the town.

After a full day of watching polar bears we visited a First Nation lady who showed us her arts and crafts and told us some interesting history of her people. She said that they were called Indians when the Europeans first landed in Churchill. But they were not from India. So, they called them Red Indians, which was also not right. Then they called them Eskimos and now finally they are called "First Nation" people. "Inuit" are from one of the tribes of first nation people who have settled in Churchill. Another time we visited the studio of a photographer who showed us some of the most amazing photographs taken throughout the year in Churchill. Through these photographs we got a good idea about the life in Churchill year round. The photographer showed us the photographs of Northern lights which inspired me to return to the Arctic in winter months.

We visited Eskimo museum, one of the finest I have ever seen. The craftwork done by these people was unbelievable. They showed us fine details of their life experiences through their arts and crafts.

On the last day we went on dog sledge ride, which was the epitome of excitement. The "Big Dog" as he called himself was an engineer. He did dog sledging as his hobby. He had several dogs in his huge yard. He described to us how he trained and nurtured his dogs. The dogs that led the sledge were called leads. He described the orders he gave them to slow down, to not get distracted by the squirrels etc. I loved him say that he was their physiotherapist, massage therapist, nutritionist and so on. He clearly loved his dogs. He also participates in dog sledge races. Viren and I were on one sledge. The wind was blowing hard and it was chilling cold but it was worth it. Our adult children thought we had become adventurous by going to winter wonderlands. They did not know that their parents were exploring such adventures wherever they travelled.

Toronto: The next opportunity was to visit *Toronto* for my psychiatric conference. We arrived one day early. CN tower was right around the corner from our hotel. As we visited the tower, we saw that there was an opportunity to do the Edge Walk which is Toronto's tallest urban adventure and the world's highest full- circle hands- free walk. We went to its viewing deck at the CN tower to enjoy 360 degree views of Toronto and Lake Ontario. It looked like a dangerous and knee- shaking adventure. We considered the worst that could happen, however the imagined thrill was too difficult to turn down. We had to wear the appropriate outfits given to us by the staff. We were attached to the chains which were attached to the gear that circulated along the roof of the tower and we walked with it, totally hands free. We were a group of ten people. Viren and I were the senior most. The rest were half our age. We had not informed our children that we were heading for this adventure. But now having done it, it is easier to describe the tower's impressive height on the Edgewalk, which is hands free walk on a 1.5 meter ledge, 116 stories above the ground. The tickets were $ 225 per person which included a certificate of achievement, printed photos, a video, a Movie and Motion Theatre Ride. It was a beautiful, sunny day. The winds were quiet. We were reassured that our safety was taken very seriously. We believed them.

Our knees were shaky to start but little by little we walked all around the edge. The fear turned into thrill that words cannot describe. We shocked our children and friends when we showed them our pictures and the movie.

Polar Bears in Churchill, Canada

Polar Bears, mom and cub in Churchill, Canada

Nalini and Viren outside the first museum of Human Rights
with statue of Mahatma Gandhi, Winnipeg, Canada

CN Tower, Toronto, Canada

Europe: the Continent of Diverse Cultures

Quite some time after we moved to New York and Viren had settled in his residency training program, we realized that resident doctors received higher salaries in New York than those in Michigan. But, of course as we would soon find out, the standard of living in New York was also higher; much higher! All first generation immigrants are good at saving money and we were no different; except that we spent significant amount of what we had saved on our trip to Canada. We never regretted spending money on experiences; it had become our priority!

It was fall of 1971. The foliage was extraordinary; something I had not seen in India. We decided to travel through Europe while nature was still changing colors. The memory of our first trip to London and Paris en route to Michigan was quite fresh on my mind. It was at that time that we had decided to return back to Europe when we can take a bird's eye view of various European countries. Someone from Amsterdam once noted that the Japanese can see all of Europe in a week. "You can't even see Amsterdam in a week, let alone Europe." But this did not matter to us; we wanted to see it all. I collected a number of travel catalogues from travel agencies and began to study tours, which were offered by different tour companies. We wanted to do sightseeing, understand cultures through meeting natives and learn about different vegetarian cuisines aside from our own. We decided to take a tour entitled "European Sampler" offered by American Express.

Our trip started in *London, then to Brussels and Amsterdam, followed by a cruise through the Rhine River, winding down in Lucerne, Switzerland and ended in Paris.* We travelled along the most scenic parts of the river Rhine where foliage was at its peak. The west must have this in common, I thought. In the midst of these beautiful colors were the centuries old castles. We entered the pine-clad hills of the Black Forest, Schwarzwald as they say in German, and for the first time I saw a cuckoo clock. No, this was not some of the patients I would later encounter. I was fascinated by the cuckoo clock and its artistry by the local wood carvers. We bought one to bring home. Since then I have always had a cuckoo clock in my house. On the Swiss border we saw the Rhine falls. We entered picturesque Lucerne where I bought my first Swiss watch and tasted chocolate pralines. We did all things Swiss; naturally enjoying them!

We crossed the border into France and drove through the vineyards of Burgundy and then entered familiar Paris. Versailles fascinated me the same way the Taj Mahal did; sheer size, sheer beauty, a giant among us! But these giants are not natural; they are manmade; understanding that scale is important! We saw our first dinner and show at the Moulin Rouge. It was a total culture shock. I had my first sip of Champagne. I liked the taste but did not enjoy drinking more than a couple of sips; alcohol still was not of interest. I remember looking at the Eifel tower and comparing it again to the pictures and postcards I have seen. When something is real, it's real.

Two weeks prior to starting our trip, I reminisced on my childhood dream to visit *Switzerland* and meet Barbara, my pen friend from grade school. We both were in eighth grade when we wrote to each other about each other, about our ambitions, about my desire to travel abroad and see "what else is out there." Barbara was a friend who I had not met in person but we had developed pen friendship, maybe something like kids are doing today with their online dating apps, except this was pure friendship, not lonely isolation looking for lonelier companionship. Barbara lived in Zurich, Switzerland, and we had exchanged several letters over high school and college years. Barbara joined nursing school after college and I joined medical school. She said, in one of her letters, that her father had business contacts in India and she could arrange for me to visit Switzerland after we graduate from our respective postgraduate schools. We fantasized about practicing in the same hospital in Switzerland; me as a doctor and she as a nurse, cuckoo clocks, chocolate and all.

Soon after her graduation from nursing school she announced that she was going to marry her childhood sweetheart, Werner. She had told me all about Werner in our letters. He was an Engineer and his work assignments took him to different parts of Switzerland, he had a bit of travel in him too. The Swiss are shrewd, speaking a minimum of two, maybe three, languages. Although she had sent me her wedding picture, we lost contact after her marriage as she moved in her new home and traveled with Werner. Barbara did not write to me her new address where I could write back to her. It was isolating and felt like a loss. Right after my graduation from Medical school, I got married to Viren and we left for Michigan. As I planned for my new life in America, I packed many little treasures to bring with me. Among them were address of Barbara's parents and her photos, a portable memory of sorts. I was disappointed that I had lost contact with Barbara for almost two years.

Prior to taking our tour of Europe, I searched for those treasures and found her parent's address. I took some courage to write to her mother at her old home address. I asked her to send my letter to Barbara, wherever she was. In that letter I told Barbara all that had transpired in two years and that we were going to be in Lucerne, Switzerland. I gave her the exact dates and the name of the hotel where we were going to stay for two nights. There was nothing more that I could think of doing, but I was hopeful to meet her in person—a bit of hope, a lot of luck.

That day arrived. We came to Lucerne with our tour mates, on schedule, and checked into our hotel. Our hotel overlooked a beautiful lake. Viren and I decided to walk to the lake and admire the beauty of nature that had fascinated me about Switzerland; it was an immediate response, a reflux to the scenery. After a short walk we sat and watched people walking along the edge of the lake. I wondered, *if a miracle would occur which would enable me to meet Barbara.* Then again, I thought, *how would I even recognize her?* Although I had seen many photos of Barbara, everyone around me was a Caucasian and they all looked rather similar to my Indian eyes, we did not share the pleasures of knowing each other in person, though I knew her personally.

Then I saw a smiling woman walking briskly towards us. She opened her arms as she approached me and said, "You must be Nayna" (my nick name). We embraced tightly, as though we had known each other in person for years. Words have a funny way of connecting people more than on a superficial level. She said that she was able to spot us right away because we looked different; I can't help but think because we are brown-skinned Indians. I did not take offense to this; I knew Barbara well although we had never met in person. Barbara thanked me for writing her that letter giving her all the information about our stay in Lucerne. She told me that she had reserved a room in the same hotel for two nights so that we can spend time together. We left our tour mates for two days and did sightseeing with Barbara so that we can spend maximum time together. We went with her to Mount Pilatus, "the guard of Lucerne" by cable car. I had not set in a cable car ever before in my life, but these were fascinating experiences. Werner was traveling so we could not meet him but Viren and Barbara became good friends in no time. This experience of meeting Barbara in person was a dream comes true. Fate had a funny way of working itself out. Well, I put myself out there, and the gesture was returned. I was astonished by my pen-pal-turned-real-pal's kindness.

When we had to say goodbye, we both knew we will meet again. We both had tears in our eyes. They were tears of joy and sadness. We did not know when we would see each other again. I remembered someone had said, "*That nobody understands the reason why we meet in this life's journey. We are not related by blood, we don't know each other from the start, we lived continents apart, but nature put us together to be wonderful friends by heart.*" In that moment, truer words never said, and truer words never more perfect for the way I felt. I became convinced in the power of destiny and that miracles can occur if one has faith. There was something spiritual about it; something in the realm of the unknown and the divine!

This was indeed a dream vacation. Our tour was perfectly planned by the tour company. We were offered to visit the best places and best ways to experience a sample of Europe. We learned a lot about the historical landmarks and historical characters. Guided sightseeing helped us bond with our tour companions. We shared culture through cuisines. Our dining experiences were a true delight, and our tour guide helped us find vegetarian options while preserving high quality regional specialties. This tour was not just about getting from one place to the other but the process of getting around; learning about the history and geography, about the people. This journey was sheer magic as we encountered fascinating people and places, and a little bit of the divine.

We met one local guide though, who continuously compared Europe with America in a derogatory tone putting down Americans. She offended all of us who were travelling from America. We, all tour mates bonded even more and decided to address her attitude about Americans directly with her. In our group was a Hispanic-American couple, an African-American couple, an Indian-American couple and six Caucasian couples. We spoke many languages but that day we spoke one language, English, although with different accents. This tour guide was taken aback when she saw a large group of people who looked different but identified with each other as Americans. We did not need a spokesperson. We all had something to tell her how she had offended us, offended our country. I told her that she had a right to have her own opinion but she had no good reason to share that opinion with people who she worked for; us, the American tourists. She was amazed that Americans had something special about them that Europeans did not. We were not British, or French or Swiss or Germans. We were and are Americans.

We learned that Europeans are different, in everything that they do. As we traveled from one country to the other, we saw that people, cuisine, their language and their ways of life were uniquely different. We had respect for all of them. This tour led me to confirm my gut feeling that I had identified with my fellow Americans and the process to adapt and acculturate in my new land had deepened. Every place in Europe was something amazing, beautiful, even envy-worthy, but America has something everyone wants. I wondered if it is the *Freedom* that everyone wants!

This high level view of Europe was just a taste. We knew we will return several times to visit this continent, visiting each country at a time. How very different is each country in Europe, again something envy-worthy! A bird's eye view is only an invitation to return and tour each country at a time.

We returned, but this time to tour ***Ireland and Scotland***, and this tour was highly educational among other things. The new knowledge that I acquired intertwined politics, history, culture and the religion of its people. This tour was highly inspirational as the independence of Scotland is hard to ignore. Scotland is one of the four countries of United Kingdom. The other three are Wales,

England and Northern Ireland. These countries have their own governance but the taxes are paid to the UK. This, of course, was before England voted to leave the European Union.

In 1928, Ireland became independent of the UK, however, Northern Ireland continued to be part of the UK, and do not mix these up, you will greatly upset someone. Northern Ireland's capital, Belfast has seen bloody wars fought on its land in Derry, (officially known as London Derry) between the Irish republic and the loyalists. Currently, the population of Northern Ireland is seventy percent catholic and thirty percent Protestant. England gave land to these Protestants in Northern Ireland in the past and they have remained loyalists, however, many have immigrated to the United States, New Zealand and Australia. I had learned here in the United States from one of my Scottish friend that this second wave of immigrants was known as the Scot-Irish immigration. It is believed that these people emigrated in 1930. They brought their fiddle-style music to the United States, which became Appalachian Folk music. Today, it is known as country music.

The first wave of Irish immigrants came to the US, Quebec, and Australia during the potato famine during 1848-1852. They sailed on a ship called *famine ship*, which is located in Dublin on the river Liffey. Those who could pay the fare (one half of the average income of Irish people) at that time could purchase a seat to board this ship to New York, Ellis Island, specifically. The poor identified one member of the family who would sail while several family members contributed towards the fare. Imagine the sacrifice. This person then sent money for others to emigrate and the cycle continued. This ship sailed twice a year in April and in August.

We took a tour inside the ship. Some very meaningful posters were placed in the cabin which advised the emigrants what to expect during the sailing period as well as after they arrive in

New York. The most important message I read was that "In the US, labor was honored and there was no shame in doing any kind of labor. The person who did not find work was because of his character defect." All work is noble! Isn't this message true for every immigrant even today? It may be this wisdom that has led to the successful lives of most hard working ethical immigrants. The Scot Irish looked down upon the Irish emigrants of 1848 in the United States because they were poor farmers and of lower class in Ireland. I identified and understood the trials of Irish immigrants. The Irish have always been second-class citizens to the English and people who sympathize with the crown. They still are not fond of each other.

The paintings and posters on the walls of the buildings in *Belfast* convey strong sentiments of desire to have peace with Ireland through negotiations. There is a hope that the next generations of two countries will put their differences behind them. Northern Ireland uses British pounds as their currency while Ireland being part of the European Union uses Euros.

The Irish are proud of their culture and devoted to their country and catholic religion. *Knock, County Mayo* is a place where pilgrims visit each year from all over the world to visit the shrine where Catholics believe that revelation had occurred. An international airport has been built in *Knock*.

In addition to the castles, we witnessed the natural beauty in *Ring of Kerry, the Cliffs of Moher and the Giant's Causeway,* where the lime stone mountains and cliffs soar majestically over the rocky ocean coast below. They have taken different forms over millions of years but still shoot ominously above the cold sea below. They are also sites where there is abundance of wild life and different kinds of birds have inhabited themselves. Such emerald landscapes left a permanent impression on my mind. It really is greener than they say, and the Irish air and pace of life calms the soul and relaxes the mind.

We visited Belleek pottery factory where world famous Irish white china pieces are painted by hand. This factory was established in 1857 and continues on to the present.

They export sixty percent of their pieces to the United States and the rest, forty-percent, everywhere else in the world. All throughout the first week of our trip the future King of England, George Alexander Lewis, son of Kate and William was anxiously awaited by the English people and the world. He was born on 7/22/13. One day later, at Belleek factory on 7/23/13 the artisans were making a baby cup with the name *George Alexander Lewis 7/22/13* engraved on it. Old traditions carry heavy there, and the world respects them. We must not forget that we are not far from our colonial and imperial past. Signs are a way to tell this.

The Irish Shamrock is a sign of peace and is a true Irish symbol that we saw everywhere on various pieces of china in this factory. Irish cabaret and step dances are other cultural riches that speak volumes about Irish life. In James Joyce's *"The Dead,"* a woman scolds the main character, Gabriel, for not wanting to visit the Aran Isles, a place devoted to Irish heritage and pride. While the English strangled Ireland, this was the only place for Irish heritage in Ireland, in the Isles. Now, children take Irish in school, boys play hurling, girls' step dance. The Irish are an immensely proud people, and that could be part of the problem. Nations who fight so hard for independence have trouble moving beyond that. There even was a Charlie Chaplin statue on the resort area in Ireland where he spent summers each year. Irish summers are as pure as Irish butter; soft, warm and with a little bit of salt. In Dublin we took a tour of Guinness and learned about Ireland's famous cultural heritage: drinking. The Jameson Whiskey storehouse tour showed that the Whiskey is stored for ten to eighteen years in the large barrels.

On a darker yet fascinating note, we learned the insider stories behind the famous, ill-fated *Titanic*, designed to be one of the finest ships made by mankind and destroyed by nature's ice. It was a humbling experience to accept that human brains cannot defy the destiny created by nature. She is all powerful.

We spent a short time in **Liverpool** to visit the Beatles museum, which was fun and educational. The story that brought four guys together, the death of their manager, the parting of ways of the four guys was very touching. John Lennon was one of them. Paul McCarthy is the only survivor who has become involved in spiritual activities of *Hare Rama Hare Krishna, and yoga.* Their pictures in the museum told an amazing story of the B*eatles.*

Traveling from one country to the other in Europe is an eye opener. We arrived in *Scotland* which is a different journey: fierce and windswept. We had heard about bagpiper's poignant and eerie skirls in the United States but watching them entertaining the guests during dinner exceeded expectations. We enjoyed Scottish dances, and piper music. Although, haggies (a special lamb meat dish) are popular, we did not indulge because of our vegetarian dietary choice. We accompanied our tour mates to a restaurant where we enjoyed Scottish vegetarian dishes. We learned that Scottish kilts are culturally preserved but not worn by common men.

Scotland's capital is **Edinburgh** where out of a total of six million people, four and a half million reside in Glasgow. Overall, Scotland is quiet, with beautiful a countryside. Queen Victoria and her husband Arthur built a summer castle in Scotland where all members of the royal family continue to stay from July end to September each year, when the castle is not available to be visited by the tourists. Those days wherever the Monarchy travelled, the aristocrats followed. The country has beautiful mansions where aristocrats spend their summers as well.

The ship *Britannia* in which the monarchy travelled all over the world has now been donated to Edinburgh. Princess Diana's photo on the ship with her arms stretched out to hug her two boys is very touching, knowing her fate. It was clear from the photographs that Diana visited the sailors and the crew on the lower decks of *Britannia* frequently and they appreciated her. She was loved.

Overall this tour gave us insider pleasures on a sojourn through Ireland, Northern Ireland, and Scotland, exploring capital cities, winding through countryside roads, and medieval towns. The experience of witnessing the beauty of the Ring of Kerry and learning how Guinness is made opened up this culture to us we previously did not know. Ireland had history in every bend, and the Irish people in all their pride, continue to celebrate the very thing that was taken from them. Scotland will always be Scotland. Rugged and independent, lined with mansions and manors that remind of the past; and in between the kilts and bagpipes twirl and sing to reinforce their independence; two islands, many identities!

España

Spain had something different to it, maybe it was the history, the architecture, the people, the music, the food, the artists, the old notions of bravery and former colonial greatness, but certainly Spain had the old European charm it holds on to. Between bullfights and *Gaudi's architecture*, the magnificent *Alhambra* and the white washed villages of *Andalusia* and the magnificent artwork in the Prado Museum in Madrid, my memories of Spain will never wash away; I take them wherever we go.

We arrived in *Barcelona* and immediately I explored up and down Las Ramblas, a wide street, which has two end streets where vehicles can pass and a wide center area where people walk up and down the street from dawn to late nights. I find Europeans walk much more than Americans. It ends on the Mediterranean Sea where the bars, restaurants, and shops make La Ramblas lively. The central area with ice cream and vendors is excellent while sitting on benches and *"people watching."* I suppose I don't find this abnormal, since my day job has been to *"people watch"* when they seek my help for emotional difficulties. People always fascinate me, without them, a region is nothing.

On Sunday we went to the cathedral to watch groups of people dance outside to celebrate and pray. Groups of seniors as well children danced together, and we thought that this well-known activity every Sunday morning was wonderful because it brought families and communities together. It was hard to tell how many of these people were church-goers, but one thing was for sure that everyone was having a great time. This kind of relaxing atmosphere that brought out warmth defined Spanish culture for me. If you were to ask a Spaniard what religion they are, they would say, "catholic."

To enjoy the architecture in Spain one has to walk and admire the thirteenth to twentieth century cathedrals, royal Palaces, bell towers, museums and plazas with fountains. They knew how to fancy royal delights. You could photograph everything. I became obsessed with photographing everything and, in fact, I took over a thousand pictures in one week. I loved to watch these pictures over and over, perhaps the best way to keep the memories alive.

The architect, *Antony Gaudi*, whose name is synonymous with Barcelona, has designed masterpieces of nineteenth and early twentieth century. *Parc Guell, a palace designed by Gaudi and El Temple Expiatori de la Sagrada Familia,* an unfinished cathedral featuring three different facades, each with four finely detailed intricate spires and a dome that towers over five-hundred feet are the most amazing places to visit.

We visited the *Picasso museum*, which can be accessed through very narrow streets where hardly four people can stand in a row. These narrow streets are lined by Tapas bars, ice cream stands, boutiques and souvenir shops. The Spanish could pack it all into an alley way. Small alleys are one of my favorite things about old cities. *Sagrada Familia* will be fully completed in 2026. I knew I will be eighty years old, if alive, and most likely will not be able to visit myself. I suggested to all my children and grandchildren to put this place in their bucket list. Although I do not qualify as a professional photographer, I am very happy to have taken some unusual pictures inside and outside of these masterpieces.

Aside from the larger cities like Barcelona, Seville, and Madrid, Spain offers an insight into its historical past through smaller cities like *Ronda, Granada, and Cordoba*. Meals at historic sites such as Parador Ronda made this trip special and even like time travel. Ronda provided a trip into Spain's Moorish past since it was the last city that fell to the crusaders. The cliff top Ronda has indeed its veiled beauty. Many Diasporas started here.

Walking up and down the hilly cobble stoned streets, I noticed a small window at the street level where a well-dressed woman in her eighties was sitting and watching people, like me; many of them tourists. I could see only her face up to her shoulders, almost like a framed picture. My eyes met hers. She acknowledged me with a warm smile and twinkle in her eyes. This moment was very special. I wanted to carry this experience with me through photography. We did not communicate; we did not have a common language to talk. Her smile was fixed on me as if she did want to say something. We were only a foot away from each other. I gathered some courage and in a makeshift sign language asked if I can take her photograph. She nodded and I clicked the photo. Then in the next moment I thought I should share this beautiful interaction through the photo with her. I pulled up her photo in my camera and passed it through her 3x3 window, her own frame. She looked at it and her beautiful smile spoke more than a thousand words that she liked it. She gently passed my camera back to me. I smiled and then she smiled. I snapped out of that momentous time spent with her and noticed that the rest of my tour mates had moved on. I said "gracias" in Spanish since that was the only word I could find in my limited Spanish lexicon; I was choking and unable to express my emotions in any other way. In a panic state I left her, knowing I will never see her again but her memory has stayed on with me. This photo, the loving moment I spent with a total stranger, and the nonverbal communication we shared will always stay with me as the memorable event of this trip to Ronda, Spain.

Plaza de Toros, a historical bull fighting ring made famous in the eighteenth century by legendary bull fighter, Pedro Romero, brought out mixed emotions. Traditionally, the bullfight ends with the death of the bull. The bull gives up his life for the entertainment of thousands, as if he has a choice. I learned that the bull breeder knows his bull as well as the bull's father and grandfather. He knows its likes and dislikes and clearly loves his bull. I never got the answer to my question about how its owner raises a bull and then sends it to its death. The bullfighter is most of the times the winner displaying both the ears of the bull while parading through the town. The town people eat the bull's meat. I have chosen a vegetarian life style for the compassion towards animals and being nonviolent towards them, but I respected their culture and tradition, and I must say, in all my disagreement, there was art and bravery.

Another memorable site is the *Alhambra Palace located in Granada*. Moorish rulers built it and you can tell with all the geometrical designs. The well maintained grounds and terraced gardens once again fascinated me. I wanted to carry them with me through my photographs. Although I snapped many pictures; they do not give justice to the exquisite beauty of landscaped gardens. It has an ethereal sense of peace.

Back again to the history dating back to nearly two-thousand years, was the spectacular **Seville** which we loved. In its cathedral rests Christopher Columbus who discovered America. Although he was of Italian decent, it was the Spanish queen who sponsored his explorations. Columbus Day is called Indigenous Peoples Day because Columbus and his men raped, enslaved and murdered the natives they came across. But here in Spain where his corpse lays, it is the third largest Roman Catholic Church in the world.

Next we stopped in **Cordoba**. We visited the third largest mosque in the world, *La Mesquita,* an architectural masterpiece built in the eighth century. Here a cathedral was built within the mosque. It is heartwarming to see that they continue to co-exist, and such history and beauty co-exists.

Our last stop was *Madrid.* It reminded me of the modern cities like New York with all its hustle and bustle. The highlights of Madrid included opulent *Royal Palace built in the eighteenth century, Neptune fountains, and one of the most renowned museums, Museo Del Prado.*

Vegetarian Food in Spain continued to be a challenge for us. Risotto, Batata tapas and salads were the only vegetarian options we had. Spaniards eat large portions at lunch, take a siesta and eat late dinners. Spaniards also eat a tremendous amount of pork. We had to change our meal times to be compatible with our timings at home. We realized that the vegetarian food that we did find was without the spices that add flavor to the food. Sure enough, the satisfaction of eating came with Indian food that satisfied our Indian palate; Indian food in non-Indian places, it always gives us a kick.

Our journey to explore different and fascinating countries in Europe was never ending. We thought it was time to take tours, which take us into unusual places to watch incredible beauty of nature. We focused from culture to nature, and what we noticed is that they are connected. We had crossed the Arctic Circle three times; once to watch the Midnight Sun in Barros, Alaska. We were there at the right time to be able to watch the midnight sun. Second time we crossed the Arctic Circle when we went on Polar Bear excursion. This was the third time all along the coast of **Norway** in a cruise ship, which took us further north of Arctic Circle. This was an adventure to watch the Northern Lights!

I had seen pictures and read about the Northern Lights but to watch these celestial fireworks of nature was an out of this world experience; I needed to see it for myself! The timing to watch the Northern Lights has to be right. We were hoping to watch the Northern Lights on our excursion to watch the Polar Bears but that did not happen. My research showed that Iceland, Norway, and any lands north of the Arctic Circle will be the places to watch the Northern Lights. These places are known for the possibilities of watching the Northern Lights when the sky lights up in the most amazing colors (green, purple and red).

We were ten couples who had met for the first time and four friends who had planned this trip with each other on this cruise. Anxiously we waited day after day for the Northern Lights to show up. It was second to last day but we had not been fortunate enough to see these lights. It was dinnertime; dessert was served when an announcement came through the speakers of the dining hall that the Northern Lights were visible. Everyone ran out to go to his or her cabins, dress quickly in warm clothes and out on the deck of the ship to watch the lights. We saw some gray and white streaks but not really the colors that I had seen in pictures. Most of our cruise friends left and went back to the dining room. However, there was a family from Malaysia looking through their DSL camera with tele lens mounted on a tripod. My husband and I wondered what they were watching. We approached them and stood right next to them. After a few minutes one of the three men turned to us and said, "Do you want to see the picture I just took?"

We could not believe these were the Northern lights, which were visible only through his camera with the lens. My husband became suspicious that he was showing us some pictures that were already on his camera. He turned back towards us and said, "Do you want to watch from my camera?" Yes, indeed the lights were there. We were so warm in happiness that the bitter cold was not felt. We stood there for forty-five minutes taking turns to look through his camera and see the dancing lights. We shared our hand warmers with this family so that we all could continue to stay out in cold longer and enjoy this beauty of nature. We had bonded over nature's lights.

They promised us to share the pictures taken by their camera. We separated that night with gratitude and beautiful memory. Although we never met again during the next 24 hours before our cruise ended, we certainly received the pictures of Northern Lights that they had promised us.

Travels can take people to not only different lands but it connects people who have never met and perhaps will never meet again.

Portugal: This was a short tour of Lisbon, capital city of Portugal, located on the crisp Atlantic Ocean. Portugal was a powerful maritime empire in Europe. Its architecture dates back to 1500s and intricate design on tile work is everywhere. It is a city of gothic grit and glamour. We visited its golden beaches and ate in one of the sea side restaurants, which usually serve amazing fresh fish––so I'm told. The owner of the restaurant was of Indian origin. He enlightened us of its history and correlated it with the arrival of Portuguese people on the west coast of India. In the south western city of India, we have visited Cochin. I remember that the descendants of the Portuguese people who have merged with the main stream have preserved their presence and culture.

Eastern Europe: Warsaw, Poland, Budapest in Hungary, Prague in the Czech Republic: This was the most tremulous emotional tour. It started in Warsaw, Poland. But within the tragedy of what we saw, the human spirit's resiliency prevailed. Although 80% of Warsaw was destroyed in World War II, the city has been rebuilt, reborn, whatever you want to call it. The tour guide was however keen in showing us the pre-war historic buildings on our walking tour through 13th and 14th century old town and paintings and sketches restored to its best. On our bus tour through the

Polish country side, we arrived in *Cracow*, once the capital city of Poland. We did not have much time to spend in Cracow. We arrived at the poignant memorial and museum at *Auschwitz,* forty miles southwest of the city for a guided visit. The experience of walking to the gas chambers and stories that I heard from the tour guide were beyond belief. I followed the footsteps to death that many took, and although I have read and watched movies about Holocaust, this experience saddened me tremendously, you could feel it. We saw the train tracks on which the trains loaded with Jews were brought in for extermination. As I write this memoir, my memories of the visit to Auschwitz bring tears to my eyes. This place was the *"Final solution to the Jewish question in Europe"*. We heard this Nazi's euphemistic phrase which to this day gives me goose bumps. We saw the special badges given to enemies imprisoned in Auschwitz to mark them out: yellow stars for Jews, brown triangle for Roma (Gypsies) purple triangle for Jehovah's witnesses, black triangle for people with mental illness, prostitutes and other such minorities. It is a stark reminder that there is evil in the world. Yes, a medical definition can explain some things, but we have to remind ourselves there is evil.

As a religious vegetarian that respects all life I cannot stand the idea of destroying life. Here we heard and walked through areas where such inhumane mass killing had occurred. Evil manifesting in humankind can never be forgotten. It may even bring a necessary caution to your world perspective, but not fear. Fear is what terrorists want, fear will make you succumb. Caution will not. But, if there is a fearful thought inside you, that thought will float out of the gas chambers and into your lungs and make you ask, *"Can this happen again?"*

Although physically we left Auschwitz, emotionally I was stuck in a time when I was not even born yet. I was empty emotionally and my soul was hurting deeply. It took me days to fully move on with this tour, I walked around like a zombie, feeling the weight of evil and the weight of failure. That thought I could not seem to shake, and I do not think I ever will.

Our bus tour continued on to **Budapest in Hungary**. Our hotel was right on the Danube River which divides Budapest into two areas, Buda and Pest. Its 19ᵗʰ century chain bridge connects the hilly Buda with the flat land of Pest. We walked around in the Trinity square where 13ᵗʰ century Matthias church is located. I was reminded of my first encounter with a Hungarian friend, Margot. I met her in New York City. We lived in the same building and over time we became close as a family. They offered to be the God Parents of our oldest child, Manisha. They were Christians and we were Hindus, however this divide along religious line did not take away the sentiments that lied underneath this offer. We felt Manisha was honored by their love and sense of responsibility they were about to take.

Margot and I had talked about her experiences in Hungary, the civil war, her escape to Austria as a teenager leaving behind her entire family, living in refugee camps and being transferred to New Zealand where she lived for years prior to arriving in the United States. My visits to all these places on the tour made all such conversations real.

Our journey continued to **Vienna, Austria and on to Prague, Czech Republic**. The castle district by the ornate Charles Bridge, lined with statues centuries old made lively by artists, and musicians. I was amazed watching the *Astronomical Clock* in the old town of Prague. This clock is 600 years old and one of the most popular tourist attractions. The clock's main function is to depict the movement of the celestial bodies; the sun, moon and the stars. Since 1948, the bell and drum mechanism are set to chime on the hour according to the Central European time. It reminded me of the *Jantar Mantar* monument of Jaipur, Rajasthan, India where there is a collection of nineteen architectural astronomical instruments built in the 18ᵗʰ century.

As an American of Indian origin, I was grounded in the astronomical ways of thinking and belief system. I was named based on the astronomical chart showing the positions of the moon, sun and the stars.

Overall, this tour was emotionally stirring while visiting historic sites throughout Warsaw, Budapest, Vienna and Prague. All these sites are inextricably linked to Jewish heritage. It offered a chance to reflect and remember our own responsibility to prevent such atrocities and ultimately be weary of evil.

When we thought about touring Europe, we did not realize how incredibly different each country was! One can theoretically spend a life time of exploring this continent and still not have enough. I was content for the time being. My craving to visit the rest of the world was insatiable. The proximity of Middle Eastern countries to Europe, the history of the two and totally diverse cultures and religions was fascinating. I wanted to delve further to experience the connectedness.

Egypt: Although located in the Middle East, it is a place to discover *yesterday* and create memories for *tomorrow* while gathering impressive and vibrant experiences of *today*. I had heard about one of the wonders of the world, the *great pyramids of Giza in Egypt*. It was my desire to visit these historical pyramids some time in my life.

It was 1980s, while working on continuing medical education (CME) program at my hospital I had met the director of CME at our medical school, Albert Einstein College of Medicine. During a discussion on CME programs outside of the USA, he asked if I could direct the CME program in Egypt and organize a group of doctors who were interested in the CME tour to Egypt. I was never offered such an opportunity. I was excited and concerned because I had no experience of organizing such a trip. After consulting with Viren, I accepted the offer.

We visited the Great Pyramids of Giza. We met several

children who were climbing up the barren trees of the desert and giggling at the tourists. I asked one of them what were they thinking about the toursists who had arrived in buses to visit this great monument. He replied that there was nothing up at the top of the pyramid but these tourists climb up hundreds of steps to go and visit an empty place. He was right, but he did not know the incredible history tracing back to 5000 years. We came face to face with the pride of the Pharaohs who created this history on the grandest scale.

Some of these boys knew that the tourists like to take with them some souvenirs from this place. One boy had a face of a pharaoh made from the stone. It was made rugged to resemble what it was like when it was inside the pyramid. He tried to convince me that this piece was 5000 years old. Obviously, I did not believe him but I did like the idea of taking back home a replica. I started to haggle with him. Some young children who had accompanied their parents on our trip were excited to see how I was haggeling with the vendor. We all laughed, some mimicked my words all throughout our travels on the bus. They became my followers when we visited the Egyptian bazaars.

We took a cruise on river Nile. I took notes of fascinating Egyptian lore to discuss with my CME doctors group. We saw one of the massive rock cut temples at *Abu Simbel* near Aswan, built by Ramses II to honor Nefertari 3000 years ago. This Nile temple was constructed in the name of love. Down river in *Luxor* we saw monument that recognizes an empowered woman who outshone men more than four thousand years ago. Queen Hatshepsut dressed like a king was buried in the *valley of the kings.*

We had lively discussions as part of our CME program. We discussed some of the cultural aspects of how medicine was practiced in such a historical place 4000 years ago. We also discussed issues in the US where women were not yet empowered to become the president of the USA while a woman was accepted as a Queen in Egypt, although she had to dress as a king.

Morocco: Our tour continued its journey to Morocco, what some people call fake Africa. But Morocco is not that, it is Morocco. Located at the footsteps of Europe, Morocco is the mystical, and forever fascinating country located in Africa with the mix of Arabic and European cultures. We visited *Rabat*, the capital city on the sea side with a nice blend of French colonial architecture and Moorish style palaces, Islamic ornaments and exquisite formal gardens. The souks and the aromatic bazaars of ancient *Fez* are 1,200 years old but well preserved. The local cuisine had delicious food to please our vegetarian spicy palates. We visited the *majestic Hassan ii Mosque built on a cliff overlooking the Atlantic Ocean in Casablanca*. This is the largest mosque in the world with room for 100,000 worshippers. It has a 210m minaret topped with lasers directed toward Mecca. We learned with disappointment that the movie Casablanca was not based on Casablanca the city and it was not filmed in Morocco. But the surrounding beauty was enough to distract our disappointment.

We visited *Marrakech* and its unbelievable tabletop belly dancers, and live music in the restaurants. The food was delicious Mediterranean and experience exquisite. I could quickly get used to the Mediterranean life.

Dubai and Abudhabi : I visited Dubai and Abu Dhabi enroute my annual journey to India. It was short but very impressive trip. This place has ancient history as well as the most modern architectural marvels. Old Dubai offered cultural sites where spices, dates, dry nuts and gold souks (markets) were in abundance. We took a jeep 4X4 ride out to our desert safari in the country side. The desert was vast and I got an experience of a life time.

The modern Dubai and Abu Dhabi which is the capital of United Arab Emirates (UAE), although culturally traditional, are in the midst of building boom where sky is the limit. Falcons are the nobel birds which were historically used for hunting and continue to be used for the same reasons today. Architectural tour of *Jumeriah*, man made Palm Island entirely reclaimed from the Persian Gulf, shaped like the palm tree are some of the facsinating things of the modern era

We ascended to the observation deck on the 12 th floor of the 160 floor *Burj Khalifa*, currently the tallest building in the world. We were able to catch the amazing sights of the sea and the sunset. Dubai Mall was another extraordinary place to be where there is an indoor ski place. The Arab men and women are spotted in their native outfits as well as wetern outfits. The stores that we visit in the USA can be found in the Dubai Mall. Food was a delight in Dubai and Abu Dhabi. We enjoyed the Falafel, salads and Indian food which was also available every where. The labor class in UAE is from India, Pakistan, Philipines and some African countries. I learned that in UAE the labor comes with a contract. When the contract is completed the laborer must go back home. Government has documents which show when the laborer is expected to return back to their native place. There are no illegal aliens in UAE and anyone is found illegally in the country, they are imprisoned and being imprisoned in UAE is no picnic.

In **Abu Dhabi,** we took a tour of the newly opened *Sheik Zayed Grand Mosque* whose grandeur can only be experienced. We had to provide our passports for identification and dress in the local outfit which included a long gown with a cover for the head. There are seven chandeliers with millions of Swarovski crystals. The center chandelier is considered the third largest in the world. There is an immensely beautiful Persian rug unrivalled anywhere else.

We visited the *Miracle Garden* in Dubai. It is a flower garden. There are 45 million blooming flowers all showcased in a variety of immense sculptures and designs ranging from arches, cars, umbrellas, hearts, pyramids, stars, igloos, just to mention a few. This place took my heart away. It was more like an immersive art exhibit, a true miracle, a magnanimous garden in the midst of a desert. I took pictures at every step in this wonderful place that I wished I could return again. I left the country with a determination to return as I was sure there will be so many new sites to visit in the future.

Turkey: Every year a travel expo is organized in the Jacob Javitz center in New York. We visited one of these expos. It was highly educational as we walked from one exhibit to the other organized by travel agencies. I met a travel agency that offered exclusive tours to Turkey and Greece.

I had seen some amazing pictures of *Cappadochia and Pamukale* in Turkey. I was truly inspired to visit these natural sites. This travel agency was impressed that we wanted to take a rather unusual tour of Turkey. They were willing to custom make the kind of tour I had in mind. We reserved a private car with a driver and a tour guide who spoke good English.

We arrived in *Istanbul*. From our hotel window we could see the stunning strait of waters that unites the Black Sea and the Sea of Marmara and forms the natural boundary between the European Turkey and Asian or Antolian Turkey. The cultures of the two are very different. We had chosen to travel by road through the European Turkey.

The most impressive visit in Istanbul was to the *Blue Mosque and Hagia Sophia* which reflect a melting pot of Muslims and Chritian culture. They are two of the architectural maser pieces in Istanbul. Blue Mosque has six minarets and cascading domes and the ceiling lined with some 20,000 tiles of blue Iznik design. I love to collect tiles from places I have traveled and use them to cover table tops to remind me of the stories behind each of these tiles. The grand bazaar was truly amazing. It is one of the world's oldest covered markets in the world. There are thousand of shops, mosques, Turkish baths, fountains, and cafes within the mall. We took a guided tour of *Topkapi Palace* which is now a museum.

We visited a restaurant which demonstrated to us how flat bread with stuffing was made. We asked if the chef could make this flat bread with vegetables since we did not eat chicken, meat or fish. The chef was very willing to improvise and create a stuffing with spinach and cheese. This was a delicious local meal which we will remember for ever. This chef asked us to visit the restaurant every day throughout our stay in Instanbul. She wanted to create more interesting vegetarian stuffing for the flat bread. We were touched by her expression of love to feed us. Sure enough, we visited every day to enjoy a new delightful meal and the love with which it was served to us.

We left Istanbul by car. Soon after we visited *Pamukkale,* the Turkish name which means *"Cotton Castle"*. I had seen the most amazing pictures while surfing the web and Pamukkale is a town in western Turkey, known for its mineral rich thermal waters which deposit white calcium and other minerals while flowing down terraces on a nearby hillside. In pictures they look like white snow deposited on these terraces. But in reality it was water. I took pictures while walking on the white land through the mineral waters without any shoes. Viren began to experience painful feelings in the soles of his feet due to the rugged land underneath. We heard that the soothing baths in Pamukkale hot springs with mineral water were used to treat skin diseases and for arthritis. It has historical significance as well. An ancient Roman city was founded around 190 BC. We saw an antique pool famous for its submerged Roman columns, as a result of an earthquake.

Our scenic drive by car brought us to *Konya, the resting place of the Sufi poet Jelaluddin Rumi (1207-1273).* He founded the spiritual part of Islam, Sufi, which helps develop spritual growth through poetry, music and dance. We visited the Mevlana complex with green dome mausoleum where Rumi is entombed and learned about the famous Rumi's teachings. We watched a show performed by the *whirling dervishes*, a sect that strives for spiritual growth through music and dance. It was performed in a rock cave which was interesting.

Our next destination was *Cappadocia*. We were amazed to see hills where myriads of tunnels and dwellings were burrowed. It has been believed that the early pagans had fled here to escape persecution by the Romans. These dwellings have paintings which tell stories of their lives at that time. We visited one such family's dwelling which was amazingly modern. They had modern appliances such as a refrigerator, and an oven, but they had continued to live there and tell the stories of their ancestors and maintain their culture.

Israel and Palestine: Flight to Tel Aviv was unlike anything I have ever encountered. Most of the people on our flight were Jewish. In the early morning ten orthodox Jewish men stood up and wore a black ribbon on their heads and left arm. There was a small book tied on their forehead. They said that the ribbon connected their hearts to the heads, and their heads to God. They had beige shawl that they wore over their shoulders across their backs with black stripes at the end of the shawl. These men stood facing Jerusalem in the corner of the plane and prayed for 15 minutes. We learned this information from a man who teaches language and religious studies in Michigan sitting next to us on the plane. A chance encounter I suppose. I was captivated, but did not want to disturb these men. I wondered what they were praying towards. I remembered those devoted Muslims who also stretch a piece of cloth on the ground wherever they are to pray five times in a day. They face Mecca as Jews face Jerusalem.

On the next day we arrived for a welcome dinner at the hotel and met our tour companions. Several of these companions were from the United States. One of our traveling companions took a picture of the United States flag at half-mast. The Israeli police and the American security detained him for one hour and after questioning released him. Although we were told that you can take pictures anywhere in the country, we learned that it was important to use proper judgment when rules in different parts of the world are different. Freedom is defined differently as well.

Tel Aviv is a modern city and young people's hub—it is the city Israel built. Our hotel was right on the beach, another Mediterranean coast, and we travelled through the areas where the biblical tail of David's victory over Goliath occurred. Though there are occasional stabbings and shootings, Tel Aviv is very safe. People are walking around until late night, restaurants and bars are open and crowded by young people. It is another city that does not sleep. People always seem to be celebrating something. Our bus tour drove to *Jaffa* to see the port on the Mediterranean Sea where at night deaf and blind people perform on the stage. We went to *Caesarea* where the history of the Romans and the crusaders is depicted. Movie Ben- Hur was filmed here in the amphitheater. The construction, destruction and reconstruction were the overall theme of this area. Once again the resilience of people amazed me!

We visited *Cana,* where Jesus converted water into wine at a church wedding. This was a miracle according to some scripts dug up archeologically and preserved in the church of Cana. People come here to renew their vows. This is where seven couples from our group renewed their vows. The ceremony of 15 minutes was simply beautiful.

I took pictures for these couples in their cameras. They were very grateful since this will be a memorable event for these Christians. Then we saw the sight in *Nazarath* where the angel brought Emmanuel (one who is near God) to Mary and Joseph. This was the site where 70 families lived at the time of Jesus. From there, we descended. We travelled 700 meters below the sea level. The scenery of the mountain Cameron, the Sea of Galilee, the Jordan River, the greenery, flowering trees with orange, purple and fascia colors all over astonished me as I thought of Israel as the desert.

We checked in a hotel named *Kibbutz Lavis*. It is run by families who live in a Kibbutz on the same grounds. They gave us a lecture given by a man who lived in Kew Gardens, NY prior to joining Kibbutz life in 1968. Kibbutzim were very popular from 1910 – 1970 when Jews slowly left Europe for *Ersatz Yisrael* (Greater Israel). Those Jews that escaped Europe and arrived in Israel were illegal and homeless. Israel was a colony of Great Britain at that time, and the British gave this land to the Jews. There were no jobs and survival was challenging. But the Kibbutzim—essentially an agricultural commune—brought community life where all Jews, young, old, strong, weak, women, men, together fortified themselves as a strong, cohesive unit. They worked together, they ate together, and the families had separate lodging.

We met a lady who came from London. She is trained to be an educator and she has a job with Ministry of Education on a part-time basis. She said that Kibbutz living is not very simple to understand. It requires a mindset that *"if I can survive but don't have more it is ok because when a group does well I do well as well"*. In Kibbutzim, people do all kinds of jobs within and outside of Kibbutz. Everyone's earnings are given to the Kibbutz. Every family gets some money based on the size of the family. All household chores are done by people who do household work. Everyone eats together. She said that although in Kibbutz no one has too much, no one goes hungry either. Kibbutz is governed by democratic committees. Elders are respected and taken care of, so are the very young who go to day care and those up to the age of 14 attend kibbutz school. Initially there were no distractions in Kibbutz such as TV. But now they have many such technological tools. She told us that now situation has changed. People are more settled, feel more secured and want to have capitalistic society.

We arrived in Jerusalem where Jesus spent his final days on earth. Friday is a half-day of work in Israel since Muslims and Jews prepare for Sabbath. In Jerusalem, streets in the evening are full of people who walk to the *Western Wall (Wailing Wall)* to pray. Jews have poured their heartfelt prayers to God at this site. Thus it became known as the Wailing Wall. It is the most famous pilgrimage spot in Jerusalem. Judaism, Christianity and Islam have been battling for this site for more than 1000 years. Men and women are separated by a wooden fence which is more than 100 feet long. We learned that there is a beautiful tradition at the Western Wall. People write a prayer on a piece of paper and stuff it in the crevices of the wall. Every few days a caretaker collects and buries them on the Mount of Oliver in a 2000 year old cemetery. Thus it becomes an eternal prayer. This was the site where those men on the airplane were praying to.

After dinner, we went with 15 of our travel companions to see the Western Wall. One of our companions, Anna, from Chicago, was Jewish of Russian descent. She had the idea to walk up to the wall but did not know directions.

I stopped by the front desk of the hotel, got a map and received some vague directions like "three lefts and a right; go all the way to Jaffa Gate and ask someone".

"How much of a walk is that", I asked.

He said, "About twenty minutes".

We had the courage and the rest all followed. We did not know how to communicate in Hebrew and finally we asked a girl walking by herself, directions to the wall. She said that we were on the right path. We saw several orthodox Jewish people walking in a group in the opposite direction than us. They looked like they were returning from the wall. We continued to ask for directions and we were reassured that the wall was within another twenty minute walk. By now we had walked for over half an hour. We were hysterical about what a twenty minute walk really meant in this country. We continued in the direction from where people were returning. Finally, we reached the wall. Men and women from our group had to go from two separate entrances. We prayed at the wall for peace. People wrote notes and placed them in the crevices of the wall. It was an emotional moment for many of us. It was inspiring to imagine that civilization developed from these cracks.

Finally, we realized that we had to go back to the hotel but did not know the way since we had followed other people who were heading to the wall. We saw a man in army uniform. When we asked him how to reach Jaffa Gate, the only marker we had, he pulled out his GPS, I started to write down the instructions he gave us.

Anna said to the man, "Are you Russian?"

He said "Yes".

They started to talk in Russian and we immediately knew he would put us on the right path.

This was the power of familiarity. Language had bonded total strangers. We walked but after a while nothing looked familiar. We saw a young lady and a man walking and speaking a language that sounded like English. She was from San Diego and he was from Boston. Dave from Michigan, a tall funny man from our group stepped forward and asked how we could reach Jaffa Gate. There was an instantaneous friendship as we were from the same country. We all followed them; we could trust them. Now we were a group of 17. They took short cuts through small alleys where there was not a single soul on the road. These two companions said that it was an Arabic market place which was closed at night and turns into pubs and bars. We reached the Jaffa gate where our companions parted. Now we scratched our memory to reverse the path back to the hotel. We laughed hysterically at this adventure. It ended up being a three mile walk. Finally, we returned back to the hotel. It was a spiritual experience to pray at the first temple of David at the wall. It was a great bonding experience with a lot of laughter and fun. We visited the *church of Beatitude* where Jesus gave 9 sermons to his disciples. Pope Francis the second had visited this church during the same week when we were in Tel Aviv. I felt special to visit the same church where Pope Francis had just visited.

We saw the ancient *Galilee Boat*. In 1986 when the water of the sea Galilee had receded due to severe drought, this vessel which was buried in the sea-bed was excavated. It was dated to first century BC, and believed to be used around the time of Jesus. This boat is preserved in the Galilee museum. We took a forty-five minute boat cruise on the Sea of Galilee. These boats are prepared in the image of the ancient Galilee boat to give that authentic feel we pay for.

Our wedding anniversary is May 31. That day we went to the *Dead Sea* which borders Israel, the West Bank and Jordan. This place was in my bucket list for a long time but I was not prepared to visit Israel when it was politically unstable. Dead Sea is a salt lake whose banks are 400m below sea level, the lowest point on dry land. Its famous hypersaline water makes floating easy and its mineral rich black mud is used for therapeutic and cosmetic treatments. Just do not enter the water if you have any cuts, scrapes, diaper rash or anything like that. You will regret it.

It was an experience beyond belief to have the feeling of buoyancy. When the water touched my face, I tasted salt and in a second it dripped down my face getting into my eyes. This was such a burning feeling that immediately I had to wash it off my body before going back again in the water. I scrubbed black mud from the Dead Sea on to the entire body. After spending about an hour on the mineral beach of the Dead Sea it was time to leave. I left with a wish to return back some day in future. The minerals and the mud from the Dead Sea are used to prepare cosmetics and chemical treatments which are used for treatment of arthritis, skin diseases such as eczema and psoriasis. Everyone who visits this area goes home with these cosmetics.

We also visited *Masada* which is currently inscribed on the

UNESCO world Heritage List since 2001. It is the third most visited place by the tourists who visit Israel. It is a rugged natural fortress of majestic beauty in the Judean Desert overlooking the Dead Sea that shoots up towards the heavens with mystical anger. It is a Jewish cultural icon and a symbol of humanity's ongoing struggle for freedom from oppression.

One of the first events of great revolt of Jews against the Romans occurred in Masada where Jewish rebels had fled after the fall of Jerusalem. Roman troops made a siege wall and a ramp made of earth and wooden supports. Jews who were captured were enslaved. When the hope for a better life for 960 Jews in Masada dwindled, *Eleazar Ben Yair*, the commander of Masada gave two speeches in which he convinced the leaders of Jewish community to take their lives and lives of their families rather than to live as Roman slaves. Each one of the group leaders killed nine people and then killed themselves. Two women and two children who were hiding, escaped to Rome and told Romans what had happened. This was a thought provoking piece of information. It was inspiring to learn about those people's loyalty to their land and their identity, and to reject slavery.

We learned that Sunday is the first day of workweek in Israel. It was a Sunday when we stopped at a lookout point from Mount Oliver and spent the day walking the path where Jesus prayed his last prayer before his arrest for promoting his own belief system which Romans did not approve. We stopped at the caves and temple where Mary had lived. We walked through fifteen stations where Jesus stopped while carrying the cross up to the crucifixion (Dolorosa to Golgotha). We visited the *church of Sepulcher*, which was erected over the site of crucifixion.

We then arrived at the tomb of King David on Mount Zion and walked from the upper rooms to the lowest which was a prison cell where Jesus was kept the night before he was arrested. The tour guide had all 37 of us in that small prison cell for 60 seconds in silence to experience how long that one minute felt like. We saw there a man who was walking around with long hair and long robe like Jesus. Locals said that there are people like him who say they are Jesus. This is called Jerusalem syndrome. Something the guide said is described as a mental condition. At night seven of us tour companions started to walk towards the market in search of dates and nuts which make great gifts for people at home. While searching for these gift items, we found some snack packets made by *Haldiram*, an Indian food chain. The store owner said that there were many Indians in that neighborhood. They are invited to work in Israel to take care of elderly people. We had never expected that Indians from India lived and worked in Israel. All this exploration occurred on another of our walks which was supposedly *a twenty minute walk* but turned out to be a forty minute walk. It was fun asking directions in English and receiving answers in Hebrew or by sign language.

On the last day of our trip we visited the *Holocaust Museum and Children's memorial, Yad Vashem*. Both are built to commemorate the six million Jews who were killed in the Holocaust. The children's memorial is a walk through a dark hall where millions of stars are shinning representing the soul of each child who was killed in the Holocaust. This was a heart wrenching experience, perhaps the darkest part of human history, that reminder of evil. It brought back memories of my visit to Holocaust museum in Washington, DC and our trip to Auschwitz in Poland where Jews were killed in gas chambers.

Now onto the West Bank: Here, in Bethlehem, we visited a church built on the site where the angels announced the birth of Jesus, baby of Virgin Mary. The place where Jesus was born and then taken to the courtyard where the nativity scene occurred is described here. Joseph, father of Jesus was told that King Herod, the Roman king had found out that the angels had announced that a baby was born who will be the king of people and that baby was Jesus, the son of God. King Herod had planned to kill Jesus. Joseph, Mary and Baby Jesus left Bethlehem for the desert of Sinai to escape.

In short eight days we saw several holy places visited by the Christians, Jews and Muslims. Everyone we met was striving to have peace in the Holy Land which each group claims to own. All three faiths are Monotheistic and connected through ancestry.

There were a number of inspiring episodes which enriched my understanding of history of religions and atrocities between Jews Christians and Moslems. From 1948 until now Israel has fought two wars and won. They have an identity and they are very well organized. They are devoted to each other and to Israel. All students after graduating from high school enroll in military service. Women serve for two years and men serve for three years. There are a number of Moslem Arabs who live in Israel. They are not required to enroll in the army. Palestinians are allowed to work in Israel. They can come in at 7.00am and leave at 7.00 pm. They work in agriculture and construction jobs. All street corners have cameras; however there are hardly any police or military personnel patrolling the streets.

People walk on streets alone without any fear for safety at least until 11.00 pm. Needless to say that everyone feels safe since they have training in the army at some phase in their lives. There were also cameras on every street.

As a vegetarian I can trust Arab and Israeli food because each meal has several salads with different dressings. Falafel with salads was staple food for us because the taste was never the same. Hummus, tahini sauce, hot sauce, baba ganoush, tabbouleh were always available. For breakfast there were four different kinds of white cheeses, dry fruits and nuts in addition to breads and cereals. Eating in Israel was by far one of the easiest places for us.

Croatia, *the hidden treasure of the world*: Croatia is a Central European and Mediterranean country. It has long maritime border with Italy in the Adriatic Sea to the West, Slovenia to the Northwest, Hungary to the North, Serbia to the east, Bosnia and Herzegovina to the southeast. Croatia has the shape of a Croissant. We had to travel through Neumann, Bosnia to enter back to Croatia to visit Split.

It has an amazing coastline of 5,835km, of which 4,057 km belongs to islands, cliffs and reefs. There are 1,185 islands of which only 50 islands are populated while the remaining are untouched leaving them with natural beauty. We visited *Hvar, Brac, and Korkula* on our visit to the most amazing and mesmerizing Blue cave. The climate in Croatia is Mediterranean along the Adriatic coast with warm and dry summers and mild winters.

Our visit to Croatia in September was picture perfect. A walk through the ancient cities took us back in time to the ancient architecture of the Middle Ages and Renaissance period. There are numerous extraordinarily clean beaches. We stayed at the Bellevue hotel on the beach in Dubrovnik and at the historic Hotel Park which has 100 years of prestige and status, across from the well-known *Bacvice beach in Split.*

Tourism is one of the major industries in Croatia. The locals told us that in 2017 they received 15 million foreign tourists.

Our first destination in Croatia was Dubrovnik, long been known as the pearl of the Adriatic and a designated UNESCO World Heritage site. It's natural beauty, rich history, cultural events, food and wine brings in the seductive charm. Its Mediterranean climate, coastal scenery of incomparable beauty was the powerful magnet for our mind, body and soul.

On our first full day in Dubrovnik started with the enchanting panoramic view of the Old Town of Dubrovnik, its winding roads and medieval walls. We climbed 1000 steps up the well preserved medieval wall, walked 2 miles and went down 1000 steps. It is a living museum. I left my heart in the sparkling emerald and sapphire hues of clear sky, clashing against the rocks of countless bays and coves, cliffs of subtropical vegetation. People here are sunbathing; listening to the music played by the local musicians. Traveling to the Elaphite islands we watched the orange, lemon, pomegranate, fig and olive trees. The owners of these orchards pick those fruits and sit outside their homes to sell them to the tourists. We ate the sweetest ever figs and bought homemade olive oil to bring back home. We watched many celebrities' luxury yachts just outside the old town and in front of the island of Lokrum.

Dubrovnik is a perfect combination of past, present and future of culture, heritage, and natural beauty. This was a unique experience and an unforgettable soul nurturing place.

We went on the *ship Karaka, a replica of the ship May Flower* that had landed Christopher Columbus on the soil of America, to cruise and watch the sunset.

The Plitvice lakes national parks with its constantly changing scenery, numerous lakes and waterfalls were the most favorite and heavenly site we visited. It has been protected since 1979 as an area of an outstanding beauty with 16 emerald-turquoise lakes that are connected with each other by a fabulous system of waterfalls.

It was a great feeling to learn that Dubrovnik Republic was one of the first countries to recognize the newly independent United States of America in 1776.

Dubrovnik was the first state in Europe that abolished slavery on 27th January 1416.

In 1296 the Dubrovnik Republic built a sewer system which is still in use.

Such things can be easily learned on google search these days but to hear them from the locals was very special. It connected the past to the present and that "we were there". I had to take selfie pictures in the *Blue cave* to remind myself that I was not dreaming or watching a movie. Blue cave was highlight of our tour. It is a unique natural phenomenon!

"I was there"

Since we have not watched the TV series *"Game of Thrones"* we did not take the tour to hop on the ship which is used to film Game of Thrones. Well, we have to return for the feeling of pure raw excitement to explore the streets of King's landing and sit on the Iron Throne.

One of the facts about the origin of neck-tie in Croatia was told to us by our tour guide. When the soldiers of Croatia went to war from the coasts of Adriatic Sea starting 17th century, the loved one, and a woman would tie a red tie (Croat) around his neck as a sign of love, long life and victory. This tradition started in Croatia. Today millions of men wear red tie around their necks.

Although we don't drink any alcoholic drinks, it was nice to know that Zinfandel Grapes variety comes from Croatia and its wine is well known.

Croatia is one of those must see destination that has so many stories to tell that it is almost impossible to take it all in.

We did not have problem finding vegetarian food. Every restaurant had vegetarian options on the menu. One of the most memorable experiences we had was in the restaurant Taj Mahal. It was a Bosnian restaurant although the name would indicate it is an Indian restaurant.

As we spoke to the friendly waiter we learned that the owner, a Bosnian, worked as a waiter in a small restaurant where a woman worked as the chef. He fell in love with her and together they traveled to India to visit the Taj Mahal. He promised his wife to be that he will design a unique Bosnian restaurant and name it the *"Taj Mahal"* in memory of their love. They now have a daughter who is named *"India"*. Together they own this restaurant which is very popular. We had to make reservation although it is quite a big place.

In The old towns there are narrow streets going up the hill where small restaurants with eight to ten small tables are located.

We found a vegan, a Mexican, an Indian and a vegetarian restaurant that served authentic Dalmatian food as well as fusion items.

The most interesting part of eating is the relaxing atmosphere with live music, people drinking beer and eating at ease. One restaurant had a sign" *we do not have Wi Fi, we talk to each other*". A usual table of four would have two couples, each one looking and asking what the other couple had ordered and continuing to talk about their trip, and experiences. This was the most unique and admirable experience

Barbara and Nalini in Switzerland, Europe

Nalini and Viren with Bagpipe player in traditional
Scottish Kilts, Scotland, Europe

Nalini and Viren on the Royal Yacht Britannia, Edinburgh, Europe

Nalini in Viren in Vigeland Sculpture Park, Oslo, Norway, Europe

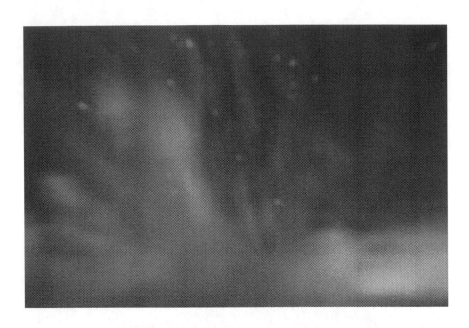

Northern Lights in Norway, Europe

Plitvice Falls National Park, Croatia

Selfie of Nalini at Blue Caves, Croatia

Nalini and Viren in Jerusalem, Israel

Within the Vast Land
of America

Prior to the birth of our first child, Manisha, in 1973, we travelled up and down the East Coast of America. We drove seven hundred miles from New York to Florida, driving through the urban and rural areas of this country. Daytona Beach was memorable not only for its clean and beautiful beaches but because on one of the beaches we accidently locked our car with the car keys inside the ignition as we rushed out to watch the sunset. We had our first experience with the kind strangers who came to assist us. One person bent his metal hanger in to a loop, passed it between the glass and the rubber of the window and pulled up the lock. The car was unlocked! Wow! We were tremendously grateful for this man's knowledge of unlocking the cars, and as we thanked him he just smiled and walked away. He did not expect anything in return. By now we had come across several such 'random acts of niceness' from local Americans. We were clearly very well welcomed immigrants. Our time to give back was on our minds. We were touched!

From Daytona Beach we travelled to Orlando and visited the famous Disney World. I felt like I was a kid all over again when we took the rides. We went down to Miami where our craving to eat some spicy vegetarian food was at its peak, and luckily we saw a pizzeria. When we entered and started to look at the menu, I saw that pepperoni pizza was available, and innocently, when we saw the word, "pepper," our taste buds salivated in an epicurean delight. We ordered this pizza, thinking it was of course vegetarian, and thinking how excited I was to have a great slice.

When our pizza arrived, we devoured all but one. It really did not taste spicy but we were also very hungry, as we ate all the slices one by one. However, Viren had some weird feeling and picked up one circle of pepper as we had expected it to be, and started to dissect it like we were in medical school all over again. He was engrossed and looked at it with the mystification as if it was the first time he held a human brain in his hands. Then, he slowly raised his head and said, *"This"* is not pepper! This is a piece of voluntary muscle." I could not believe him. I guess when you are vegetarians and doctors you don't say "meat," you say what it actually is. I frantically called the waiter and asked him about pepperoni. He explained that pepperoni was a sausage. We did not know what sausage was. He was surprised because he said that it is America's favorite food. I asked if it was vegetarian. He became serious and said "No Madam" It comes from pork and beef. When we explained to him that we were vegetarians, did not eat any kind of meat, fish, chicken, seafood or pork, he kindly pulled a chair and sat down next to us, showing us respect for the situation. This was our first blunder in this country that we ate meat without any knowledge. We felt guilty and negligent, and the waiter read that in our faces. He was very empathetic and said, "Are you vegetarian because it is your religion?" I started to explain to him that we believed that every soul was equal and that for our pleasure we did not destroy any life. He was touched by this explanation. He said, *"That is such a beautiful thought and belief."* Then he gently said, "Will your God punish you?" This amazed me, not out of horror, not of shock or ignorance, but that Christian ideology still influenced thought, and that sins are punishable. We said that we were Hindus. We believe that God is a loving God and that he/she will forgive us because we did not know what we had done, it was an accident. We will have to be more vigilant from now on and inquire every time we order anything in a restaurant. He told us about his religion and said that this would be considered a sin in his religion. He apologized although it was not his fault. We had made a stranger into a friend with whom we shared many stories about our religion and our belief system. He was very interested in learning since he said he had not met anyone like us in his past. Even though ours were different, we shared the religious experience of life together.

Our trip back home was through Blue Ridge Mountains and Luray caverns in Virginia. We went to eat in a big restaurant and ordered a vegetable platter, feeling quite confident that we had learned how to order after checking that everything we ordered was vegetarian. We had learned to be a little cautious though. I started to eat the vegetables, but they tasted somewhat different. The gravy was brown, and my suspiciousness was heightened. I called the waitress to ask if there was any meat in this order. She said, "No, all pieces of meat were taken out." Her voice was becoming irritable as our eyes were getting wider. I said, "Does that mean that these vegetables were cooked together with meat". Her voice became louder and rougher. She said "I told you already that all pieces of meat were taken out." We thought there was no point in arguing with her. We were only a "table number" for her. She could not care about the reasons why we were apparently so upset. We did not eat but paid for our food and left.

We learned one lesson, that large restaurants cannot make anything special for our needs. The waiting staff has no time to really inquire in the kitchen what was vegetarian. What a sharp contrast between this experience and our previous one, and maybe this has to do with regionalism in the United States. Miami is a vision of diaspora, a centrally blended infusion of cultures and places, and its religion is not the Americanized evangelical type, it is worldly and it is education. Now, I cannot make any assumptions about our insolent waitress, but given the area, I would be shocked if she even knew what Hinduism was. She was not worth arguing with, as I said, and it saddens me to say this, some people are often less tolerant, and less tolerant they are they tend to become more xenophobic.

After Manisha's birth we took a tour of Phoenix, Arizona, and drove up the West Coast starting from San Diego, to Los Angeles and finally to foggy San Francisco. We came across a sign for Hearst Castle in San Simeon. We decided to go up on the mountain to visit; who doesn't like castles? It was a glorious estate and looked as if God built it himself. The famous Hearst family pioneer had come to the West Coast during gold rush. During that time his wife and son travelled the world extensively and collected small and large pieces of exquisite sculptures made from marble and stones from all over the world. These pieces were carried by the mules and assembled on top of the mountain. It took twenty-eight years to complete William Randolph Hearst's lavish estate, which includes one hundred and sixty five rooms. Julia Morgan was the architect who was hired to make his dream come true. The pieces were all preserved in a castle where Hearst family visited frequently. By the time we arrived there, Hearst castle was donated to the state government and it had become California's Historical Landmark. The sole purpose of this castle was to creatively use expensive art and artifacts and display them for public admiration. The outside gardens were beautiful too with unbelievable landscaping, statues, and a huge pool. We were just shocked to see how amazing this place was. I enjoyed learning that Mr. Hearst and his mother's dream came true when their collection of Greek, Chinese, Italian, Spanish and French art was creatively used in this castle. It shows what one can achieve with unlimited resources, time and money if one has the passion for beautiful art, sculptures and artifacts. Nothing was wasted.

The Neptune swimming pool is an amazing part of the castle,

and I could not help but wonder why this landmark place was not that well known. It is indeed an amazing treasure of priceless collection of pieces of art from all over the world, all assembled in one place, but the landscape and views are magnificent. California air really does have something to it, maybe hibiscus trees or eucalyptus trees. The ride up the steep winding roads in a bus made me wonder how mules must have carried each piece all the way up on the mountain; it would have been seriously hard labor. Although, we had visited many castles in Europe, we did not know that such a beauty existed in our own country. California is God's country. The mountains fall into the sea from two-thousand meters and in return, the sea spits back its mist, its fog to wrap the eager travelers into a sleepy daze, staying drunk on the beauty that some people call home. In Big Sur, you look out onto the coast and there is nothing. Japan, maybe. The coast extends forever, and you never want to leave. It is a golden treasure, perhaps an eternal bliss. Some know it as California; others know it as home. They are the lucky ones.

All throughout the west coast we had no trouble finding vegetarian food. We had found Mexican food. We could eat many varieties of food such as tacos, nachos, burritos, enchiladas and quesadillas. We learned to order every item with beans in place of meat. Most waiting staff made efforts to understand and sometimes they educated us that some beans were cooked with pork so we must specifically ask if the beans were made with pork or they were vegetarian. The sauces were spicy and satisfied our taste buds. We became familiar with this cuisine, which then on became our favorite food in America. It had the spice, texture, and nutrients.

America is a beautiful country. It was time for us to explore our country and its heights and depths.

The National Parks:
We wanted to see the National Parks of America; The United

States has such diversity in its biomes that we wanted to see them all. We travelled by bus through four states: South Dakota, Wyoming, Idaho and Utah, and we visited several National Parks in these four states. We heard a number of inspiring stories in different parts of the park, which I have narrated here:

Badland State Park is located on a land that was formed thirty-five million years ago. As the water receded, this area we now know emerged. Large mammoths such as dinosaurs roamed this place. Currently it has the most beautiful rock dunes naturally formed and constantly changing by the forces of the wind and rain. There was tall grass called Prairie that the animals like the buffalo, bison, Prairie dog rodents survived on. This natural beauty reminded us of Cappadocia in Turkey, which is also such a naturally created place and where Pagans made their home to hide from the Romans. You could almost feel nature's cycles here, its power and its beauty.

We stopped at a place called Wall Drug. It is located in a town with eight hundred people. It is actually a huge store, which in the past was a place where tourists stopped to get free iced water, and eat. Even today the coffee costs five cents. Currently this place has many stores, a huge cafeteria that accommodates five hundred people at a time. There is a Wounded Knee museum which has Native American Indian art, crafts, jewelry, paintings, and carpets. There was a Harley Davidson store here. Every year five hundred thousand Harley Davidson motorbikes rally from Rapid City to this place and corvettes rallied as well. It was biker central and was crazy.

Our next stop was Custer State Park, which is twenty one by twenty one miles. We saw herds of Deer, Bison, and Prairie dogs and learned that there are mountain lions and coyotes in the area. We had a cookout dinner where a singer came and sang old time country songs, which I love, the kind that my Scottish friend told me about. We stayed for two nights at the Game Lodge which was the place where President Coolidge stayed during summers and called it his summer White House. Today, we visited the largest Woolley Mammoth site. It is an active site of excavation and paleontologists are working on new bones. It was an amazing experience that we were standing on the land where 27,000 years ago, such mammoths walked and fell into a sinkhole. They waited there to be discovered. They have figured that one mammoth fell in the sinkhole approximately every three months. They have already excavated three hundred mammoths. The vertebral column, ribs, femur and mandibular bones are clearly seen, and these mammoths look like elephants with long tusks, double the size and larger ears. I wonder what they were like alive and in person?

Then we visited "Crazy Horse". We heard the most inspiring stories about the Crazy Horse Memorial, which when completed will be the world's largest sculpture, a memorial to the spirit of the Native American Chief, Lakota leader Crazy Horse and his people. We looked at the picture of Crazy Horse when completed. To me his face shows the courage and commitment and his left hand is out stretched in answer to the derisive question asked by a white man, *'Where are your lands now?'* He replied, *'My lands are where my dead lie buried'.*

The Lakota chief Henry Standing Bear invited a sculptor Mr. Korczak Ziolkowski, born in Boston, of Polish descent to come to the Black Hills of South Dakota and carve a mountain. The Chief, Henry Standing Bear, stated *"My fellow chiefs and I would like the white man to know the red man has great heroes, also."* What an incredible sentiment.

The work began in 1948, and the memorial became a family undertaking as well as a humanitarian and educational public charity. Although Korczak and his wife Ruth have passed on, the work is continued by his children and grandchildren. When completed this will be the largest monument in the world. It will be taller than Rushmore and the Washington monument.

The touching part of the story was that the Native American elders wanted a red man to be remembered like the four white men in Rushmore. I agree that they deserve to be; they came first. However, unlike the organizers of the work on Mount Rushmore, the Native Americans did not accept ten million dollars of grant money from the government. Instead, the memorial is being completed with funds gathered from people's support, which conveys a great deal about the pride of the Native Americans.

I thought this is a good place to donate from our charitable foundation since it preserves the history and the pride of Lakota Indians. Here are a few touching quotes from Crazy Horse: *"My lands are where my dead lie buried,"* and, *"don't let the dream die."* These both touched my heart. What happened to the Native Americans is a true tragedy; they need memorials and a place in our history. I decided to become part of this history in making a commitment to send support for Crazy Horse every year.

We travelled through a small town of Keystone where seventy-five people live and then we arrived at the Mount Rushmore Memorial. It was a cloudy day to start but at the Rushmore Mountain there were thick clouds and fog. There was hardly any hope to see the president heads at all. I was disappointed. We watched the movie that showed the history of Mount Rushmore, took pictures of the photos thinking that this was our only hope to take back any memories. I sat on a bench in the exhibit area looking out of the window to see if clouds will thin out. Other people also sat watching. We prayed to all Gods to move the clouds, and I thought about our memorable sky ride on Hakone Mountain in Japan, where our cable car carrying all five of us had stopped and swayed with high winds that terrified us. At that time all of us prayed to Shinto God, Buddhist God, Hindu God and all Gods with a hope that we will not be stranded between two mountains, floating in the sky with a hard death below. Of course it had all ended well, and we arrived at the end of the mountain. But prayer had bonded us and relieved our anxiety through laughter.

Here also a cloud thinned and we saw outline of four heads; I screamed with joy and this hide and seek continued. Finally we walked down the trail to see the president heads. By now the clarity increased and my wishes began to come true. We took tons of pictures thinking that each one was the last one before they get covered by the clouds again. Then we took the nature trail, which offered more opportunities for viewing. Our need to take pictures from every angle at every point turned into greed, but finally contentment came as it was time to be on the bus. We missed lunch but our joy was overflowing. Food was arbitrary compared to what I had just witnessed.

We then arrived at Deadwood, a town known historically for its gold mines. Chinese and Jewish people came out here and made a little china town and Jewish people started businesses, one of them was grain mill. There were two Jewish mayors of this town. Billy Hickok, Wild Bill, was a well-known figure here for good things he did. There is a statue of him and a building where he was killed. During that time there were casinos, which still survive. It is a town of sixteen hundred people, with twenty policemen, a number of stores, hotels and restaurants. An antique store has memorabilia, which remind us of the cowboys in the movie, the *Wild, Wild West*. Everything is located on one Main Street, very typical, which is lively in summer. Then we arrived in Spearfish canyon, the most scenic area surrounded by steep mountains and a creek with waterfalls. The Spearfish Canyon lodge was beautiful, too. From the creek that drains water from the mountains is pumped through the pipes to the reservoir which provides water to the town of Spearfish. The movie "*Dancing with the Wolves*" was filmed here.

We left the Black Hills and Badlands of South Dakota and headed to Wyoming, which has half a million people and antelopes. Our lunch break was on a ranch that is maintained by a family. The husband and wife manage a hay farm that has horses, a fishing pond, and a few cottages that can be rented out to people who want to come and relax in an all-inclusive kind of a ranch resort. Vicky's mom lives with her and does laundry for the ranch and her sister comes in when she needs help in preparing all freshly made lunch for tourists like us on the bus. These two hours spent on the ranch were truly a bonus. Our bus ride was through the mountains believed to have two-hundred and fifty million years old rocks which range in color from pink, blue and beige. Big Horn mountain overlook was a stop for pictures where we met a guy named Tim who was setting up his hand glider. He would fly and land in the valley and he would find someone to drive his car down to the valley to pick up his glider again. It was fun to watch such adventurous people. I could never imagine myself doing this. Tim was brave.

We learned that National Parks are maintained for future generations while a national forest is used for the resources such as timber, mining, wood, granite, hunting and fishing etc. You can also disperse camp in National Forests. The highest point of Big horn mountain is 12,000 feet above the sea level. There are mountain lions, black bears, wolves, moose, and elks, which are spotted here. We stopped at an eatery where the best pies are made every day. We met a couple that ride a four big wheeler motorbike which, can carry three people, gasoline and food compartment. As his wife was telling me about this huge motorbike, her husband asked me if I wanted to take a ride. I said yes and as I jumped up he said, "Where is your husband?" I said he was right there with the rest of our tour members. There, Viren was coming out with his movie camera. Jim and I rode around a couple of blocks and then we returned. Some of our travel companions later told me that they were worried if they will have to start a search warrant for me if this man had disappeared with me. I never thought of it as that type of a threat, but I was flattered by the concern. Some of them took a quick picture. This was my first ride on a huge motorbike! I remembered the kind gentle man who had dropped coins in the parking meter in Michigan when I was just *off the boat* in the US. I also remembered the curious but very generous man in the restaurant who ordered pancakes for us when we had no idea what it was. We were just *off the boat*! I found there are more good people in the world than not good. Just that the good people don't make news.

The smallest town in Wyoming is Emblem, Wyoming, population of ten. They have their own post office and zip code. We also saw two wild horses, a white and a brown. They are very rarely spotted on such a tour, so we felt graced by their visit.

The town of Cody has five museums. We were able to spend two hours at Buffalo Bill Center of the West museum, it has five wings. We spent most time in learning about the life of Buffalo Bill, a charmer, entrepreneur and a free spirit who enjoyed hunting, and even performing nationally and internationally for Queen Victoria of England. He was a scout, a showman, he loved American Indians and advocated for them. After being in a circus and having produced and acted in shows he died penniless. He was married to Louisa who wanted a settled life. They had four children but two died from Scarlet fever. Eventually Louisa and Bill divorced, he was accused of infidelity and believe it or not the accused woman was Queen Victoria. They got back together after five years. He died in his sister's house surrounded by his wife and daughter. He was buried on Overlook Mountain in Denver. His funeral was fifteen miles long.

The drive to **Yellowstone national park** is spectacular. A camera cannot catch its beauty, only through the naked eye the pictures taken can be filed in the brain. Yellowstone is the first national park in the world. It is a hot spot for activities under the earth. We saw a number of hot spring eruptions with steam coming out from them. "Death in Yellowstone" is an interesting book that describes how many ways in which one can encounter death in Yellowstone. It includes falling off a cliff, scalding by hot springs, encounters with bear, elk, wolf etc. or freeze to death. We stayed overnight at Old Faithful Inn, which was two-hundred yards from the Old Faithful geyser. We watched it three times, in sunlight, in rain and at night in dark. Yellowstone is the oldest national park in the world. It has two-point-two million acres of land. We spent a whole day within the park, stopping at various overlook sites to watch the falls, scenic views, geysers, bison, elk, deer and birds. We learned about the receded ice age. Volcano and earthquakes have changed the landscape. Lots of facilities in the park close by end of September and will reopen in April. It is too dangerous to leave them open. Then came the exciting moments at dinner time when there were a number of Elks, female cow, calf and the male bull with antlers. September-Oct is their mating season. We learned that the cow comes in heat once a year and after mating she carries a scent that no other bull pursues her. She delivers a calf each year. We saw the bull pursue a cow with her calf and we followed him. There were park police all over trying to control people with cameras running to catch the event. They told us that the bull runs at 35 miles an hour speed and will throw anyone in his path using his antlers. Then there were some quiet moments. Right outside our dinning building the cow and her calf sat and across the street the bull keeping an eye on his cow also sat down. We waited outside, delayed dinner while rest of our party went for dinner. Then the cow got up and started running, the bull got up and started the chase and finally he gave up. The park service got us all inside the building. We saw three families yelling, "the bull is near the car." As he moved on the grass again the park service allowed one family with five children to cross the street. The father was walking with his eyes on the bull and shepherding all five kids and his wife in the car. They were not allowed to turn on the headlights since the light stimulates the bull. We learned that he will shed his antler in spring and they will regrow by summer again. I watched this drama from outside the building.

The next morning we woke up to see snow on the mountains around us. We went to west thumb geyser basin. There was ice as well as soft snow on the trail, which was slippery to walk but we made it all the way. Majority in our bus did not want to do it. I was able to make snow balls and bounce them in the air. We left Yellowstone Park feeling very content that we got to see and experience a lot in two days. We then drove through an entire land between Grand Teton Park and Yellowstone National Park. The Rockefeller family, while spending summers here, realized that this land will become commercialized and lose its beauty. So they established a real estate corporation, which started to buy all the land. The rangers did not like it but he paid them top dollars and finally he donated this entire land to the US government. The congress had problems in accepting this donation but finally they accepted. Today the ecosystems of two parks continue to stretch from where one ends and other begins. Rockefeller made a lodge called the Jackson Lodge, from where he sat and admired the beauty of nature. The rates for a room with the view were $339.00 per night. Today that lodge allows tourists to have lunch but the gift shop is pricey. We watched the most beautiful scenery of the Teton Mountains, Jackson and Jenny Lakes fed by the Snake River, which gets water from the glaciers. The Teton Mountains are rising while the valley is sinking. The Tetons shoot straight up to the heavens, with vigor and possibly anger. The glaciers are melting and shrinking. There are mountain climbing schools here, which train climbers to climb Mount Everest. There were tons of photo opportunities. I wanted to frame these sceneries in my brain in such a compartment that with eyes closed I could watch it again and again. The Grand Tetons give an ominous look saying, "get out." But that excited me.

Grand Teton is 13,500 feet above the sea level. We watched it from 5000 feet above the sea level. The film "Shane" was filmed here as was the film "Lewis and Clarke." We went to the town square of Jackson to enjoy the culture and visited the performing center of arts, and there was a sculpture made with blocks of wood. The artist had left several blocks for people to make their own sculptures, which Viren and I both made. This was a nice moment to share together. It was a calming experience for the mind and an inspiring idea to connect strangers. Real estate property in Jackson is very expensive because most of it is owned by the government and is preserved. We saw log homes of film stars, congressmen, and golf champion Tiger Woods. They use these log homes for three months of summer. For nine months of the year nineteen hundred people live here and over the summer ten thousand people arrive. In the afternoon we had the most exciting experience of going on the mountain by a tram, which was a twelve minute ride. We went on two trails. One of them was adventurous and one of them was not. I went halfway and Viren went to the mountain's peak while I took his movie. By this time our two cameras and one movie camera had run out of battery power. Fortunately we had captured everything we wanted, though. This adventure required a hotel shuttle, to a public bus that ran every hour to the tram station and back. A lot of coordination of timings was needed but ultimately it was a wonderful experience. We spent two hours on the mountain, had tea and met Jim and Jen from Oklahoma. They were driving their car through the national parks. They drove us back to the hotel, came in to look at our Rustic Inn located in the valley surrounded by Teton Mountains. A creek ran behind our cabins. There were swings, tepee, and rocking chairs to relax. We took many pictures with them; exchanged email addresses and parted with warm goodbyes. We went on a float on the Snake River. The ride was for thirteen miles and our guide rowing the float was Don, who was very informative. Snake River got its name from a word like a serpent that Native Indians described to the French explorers. Lewis and Clarke were French explorers whose name is used by expedition tours. Snake River has fourteen dams and it meets the vast Columbia River. We saw its canyon on our last day and we learned that Snake River canyon is deeper than Grand Canyon. The aspen trees on the banks had turned yellow and the foliage colors were exquisite.

We then crossed over to Idaho, which is famous for the Idaho potatoes, and not much else. Famous people go to Sun Valley, and Earnest Hemingway killed himself down the road in Ketchum. No one seems to know much about the scenic beauty of Idaho although one percent of Yellowstone Park is located in Idaho. We learned about Early Mormon immigrants who came from England and settled in Idaho to start. We stopped at various overlooks, the most beautiful being Bear Lake, which changes colors based on the weather. Sunny weather gives it blue color, overcast weather gives it green color and stormy weather gives its aquamarine color. We saw Logan canyon and Logan River with its delta. Lake Barnaville is a part of it which was a huge lake before the ice age. It had covered Utah, Idaho and Nevada under water. After the ice age the lake emptied and now what is left is Salt Lake.

As we headed to our final destination, *Salt Lake City* to spend the last night, we visited the Temple Square and the state Capitol with copper dome unlike gold dome that we see everywhere else. We learned that in 1847, one hundred and forty-two Mormon faith people arrived in Salt Lake City. They were immigrants from England. They tried to settle in Buffalo, then Ohio, then Mississippi and finally in Idaho and Utah. From each of these places they were evacuated at that time. Their temple allowed polygamy at that time, although it is not part of the church preaching anymore, but other communities looked down upon it then. They set up a town site, assigned a half acre site for each man, quickly planted their crops, and built their white temple.

The original person, Joseph Smith was given a message by God to be the pioneer of Mormon religion. Their church is called the church of Jesus Christ and Latter Day Saints. At that time many Protestant divisions had also occurred. Joseph Smith wanted to know the truth and this revelation had come to him. There are one hundred and forty such temples in the world. We took a tour of the temple with two ladies who were on their eighteen-month mission. It was a beautiful sight and something worth visiting. Although tourists are not allowed in the temple, we could watch a replica, which was absolutely beautiful. But you never know what is actually in the temple, and what actually goes on. Several weddings occurred in the church, and we watched a bride taking pictures on the footsteps of the church from a distance. It's hard not to smile at happiness, true happiness.

The trip ended with another adventure. Viren left his movie camera on the seat of our waiting area of United Airlines at Salt Lake City airport. We called all lost and found departments and finally found it at the airport. It was shipped to us. We believe that what belongs to us at a given time will never leave us, and what does not will have to part. We had our memories, but we wanted our camera.

Viral, Kapila, Manisha, Viren and Nalini in Alaska, USA

Nalini and Virendra at Crazy Horse Memorial to
the spirit of the Native American Chief, Lakota
Leader, Crazy Horse, South Dakota, USA

Viren and Nalini at Mount Rushmore, South Dakota, USA

My Trips to India: Home Sweet Home

After immigrating to the United States in 1970, I have taken several trips back to India, some with family and some by myself. On each of these trips I have learned something about myself, and they all have been important to me. I must admit that I miss feeding poor children every evening, bringing for them those mangoes during its peak season, and walking with them to a *Sweet Cravings* store on my birthday to have them pick their choice of sweet to eat. The joy in their eyes fulfilled me. They had celebrated my birthday, and I was beyond excited. I recognized I was a privileged child who had taken many such things for granted. In India, I had an opportunity to give back in my own way. I could not have such birthday celebrations after coming to the USA.

My initial trip was after five years of being in the United States and it was for a special reason. My grandmother, Ma, was dying from esophageal carcinoma. She had stopped eating solid food and my mother informed us that her prognosis was gleam; her doctors predicted less than six months of life. It was a short trip for a week but perhaps the most meaningful one.

I took a taxi to arrive at my grandmother's house. I was dressed in a saree (the ethnic outfit); I had long hair tied in a bun, then. I spoke Hindi with the driver as we chatted for half an hour; the time it took to arrive from the airport. He gently reminded me that women tend not to travel alone in a taxi on long drives in India.

I had become more independent after having lived in America. I had traveled through Canada and Europe. I thought about the caring comments of the senior taxi driver. This was not the country I called "Home," He had figured out that I did not live in India. What was it, I asked? Did my accent change?

He could not explain but said "*Sister, one can tell; you are not from India*".

My emotional turmoil once again distressed me. In America I was a "*foreigner*" in the eyes of the locals, although I had superficially begun to feel at home. I did not expect that I would become a "*foreigner*" in India also. I was a foreigner in both the countries. Where was my sense of belonging? I was an inside outsider.

I had to shift my thoughts from this turmoil to another one. I was there to spend meaningful time with my "Ma." Her first great granddaughter Manisha was one and half years old. Ma played with her with great delight and I experienced the joy I saw my grandmother experienced just to see us. When I left her after a week, I knew I would not see her again. I will never forget her last words that "you have fulfilled my dreams and I will always be with you as your guiding torch, for the rest of your life." What else could a granddaughter want? Tears are the only thing that happens when I think of this.

On this trip I also observed that India had become a different place all together than when I was there. It had moved on with time while I was *frozen in time* in the US like most immigrants. You imagine the place of your childhood, but it grows up just like you. India had changed and I had changed as well. I could not visualize returning back to India to settle and raise my family. This was a monumental decision for which I was determined to face any consequences. My professional and social life would be totally different if I had returned back to India. It was a tough decision which needed to be made. We decided to stay in America, become citizens and make it our home. I am happy that we did!

My next trip to India was in 1978. I was six months pregnant with our second daughter, Kapila. My sister, Niru had shared with me her secret: "she was in love." Our extended family did not support "love or choice marriage." They approved only our traditional arranged marriage. However, she wanted to get married with the love of her heart. She always looked up to me as her only sister and an older one at that: she wanted my approval. My husband, Viren, and I arrived in Mumbai with our five year old daughter, Manisha, to get my sister married. We met her chosen man and arranged for a wedding, which my grandparents, uncle, aunts and cousins did not attend. We gave her away in marriage. She was eternally grateful and very happy. We returned back to New York with a clear understanding of how families in Indian culture gave more importance to their cultural values, and traditions rather than their children's wishes. Arranged marriage was between two families and not just between a woman and a man. Those children who did not accept their parent's choice were disowned. This was the outcome in my sister's case.

Our third trip was in 1983, to fulfill a cultural, religious, traditional value of returning back to the ancestral land to offer the first loom of hair from the first haircut of a son. By then, Viral was born and he was eighteen months old. This was his first trip to India and his first haircut.

I understood from such traditions that a great deal of value was placed on continuity with ancestors and their land of origin. I thought it was worthwhile an experience for all children.

For the next six years we found it difficult to travel to India with three children. The travel time is eighteen hours and with lay overs it would be close to twenty-two hours. Secondly, our girls had great discomfort in staying with relatives in small living space, and mosquito bites, jet lag, language barrier and heat added to their discomfort especially in summer months. They were used to the American convenience of life. We had to travel during summer vacation because we needed at least three weeks to make this long trip possible. At one point when Manisha and Kapila were older, they declared that of all the international travels we had taken together, India trips were most uncomfortable. They had not seen India through the eyes of a tourist just the way they were able to experience other parts of the world.

I decided to plan two trips, two years apart, one to North India, North of Mumbai and other to South India, South of Mumbai. Each trip was planned for two weeks each, where we stayed in five-star hotels, which were converted Maharajas' palaces. We travelled to magnificent palaces, museums, historical monuments, beach resorts, temples, and to ethnic markets for shopping. All travels from *Mumbai to Delhi* (north India) and from *Mumbai to Chennai* (south India) were by airplanes and the rest by air-conditioned chauffeur driven cars. We all had a wonderful experience, which everyone remembers because they were comfortable enough to enjoy an extra ordinary beauty of nature, history, art, and early civilization of India. They wanted to return back as adults with their spouses and children. They wanted to make that connection with the land from where the first generation immigrants; their parents were born and raised. But they needed the comfort to do it.

Subsequently, several of our trips to India were to attend family weddings and some trips were to shop for ethnic clothes and accessories for wedding preparation of all our children's weddings in the US. The best place to do that was India, after all. All three of our children have married Indian spouses of their own choice and the weddings were conducted in traditional Indian ceremonies. Although I had always told them to find spouses with similar value system may that be Caucasians, Africans, Hispanics or other Asians, they all chose Spouses of Indian origin with similar values. It is gratifying to watch them pass on these values to their own children.

Since 2004, when I retired from my full time career path of a medical educator, and joined a similar educational mission with Accreditation Council for Graduate Medical Education (ACGME) on a flexible half-time basis, I have visited India every year. On some of these trips Viren accompanied me, and on some occasions Manisha, Kapila and Viral accompanied me, too. I have planned each trip in great detail so that I can obtain multifaceted experiences in limited amount of time. I have utilized portion of these trips for medical missions as well. I spend one day to meet my side of the family, relatives, especially elderly people and I spend one day visiting my husband's side of family. The rest of the time, for usually one to two weeks, I travel within India with Viren, Amta, and my relative Jyotsna or with my cousins, Manju and Pradip.

I have travelled to Jindal near *Bangalore* to experience naturopathic ways to get rid of toxicity in the body. I went to see beautiful pink city *Jaipur and Jaselmer* in Rajasthan and experience camel rides. I went to *Aurangabad* to see ancient Ellora and Ajanta caves to learn about historical aspects of century's old statues of Gods with its fine carvings and some of the destruction caused during Muslim occupation of India. I travelled to *Madhya Pradesh* to experience Tiger Safari, to *Khajuraho* where there are centuries old sensational Statues excavated from the mountains. I visited the *Taj Mahal and Swami Narayan Temple* in Delhi, all by car to experience life in urban as well as rural India. I travelled to Kerala in south India to have the experience of watching people work in tea gardens in the mountains and travelled through the backwaters of *Kerala*. It was amazing to note that illiteracy in Kerala is non-existent. Children look for pens instead of money or food from the tourists. In the early mornings, people are reading their local newspapers while having tea.

I visited several places in the state of *Gujarat*. In *Ahmedabad* during the kite-flying day, January 14, we flew the kites. The sky was colorful with all the kites and the environment was festive and enjoyable. This was Viren's childhood favorite activity. I was gratified to watch him become a kid at the age of seventy and fly kites with other fellow youngsters.

I went to *Porbandar*, land of my ancestors and birthplace of Mahatma Gandhi. I visited *Junagardh*, which is famous for its *Girnar Mountain* and lion safari in the jungles of Girnar. On Girnar Mountain there are several temples. I climbed the mountain in a doli (a chair carried by four people). I enjoyed talking to these four men who carried my chair. Three of these men reported that one of them used to drink alcohol and abuse his wife, and they felt comfort in sharing their personal stories with me and even asked me for advice. I thought these men were so innocent, open and trusting of strangers.

It was interesting to note that *Junagardh* had several boarding schools for children. I stayed in *Rajkot* for a week and shared a hotel room with my friend Meena, who lives in the USA. We both accompanied nine doctors to villages of *Rajkot and Surendranagar* to provide well children annual physical examination. I examined over thirty children a day. I was working in the capacity of a Pediatrician. This is where I met a ten-year-old girl, *Sheetal*. I sponsored her high school education after *Sheetal* told me her life story, which is similar to mine. She had lost her father when she was five years old. There was one difference though. I had grandparents who supported my higher education. I wanted to do the same for *Sheetal* and offer her an opportunity to receive education. I also observed that her school did not have pure drinking water. I installed one of those filtered water pumps for pure drinking water. These experiences were highly gratifying. Meena and I shared a room for a week. Although we have been friends for over forty years and we have supported each other through rough times, this trip thickened our friendship.

During this trip I met my distant cousins and their families in *Rajkot*. Although I used to visit them once a year every year for at least five years of my growing up years, I had not seen them or communicated with them for forty years. It was amazing to make instant connections and to talk with them about our days gone by. Some of my cousins had passed away and we talked about fragility of life. They expressed such joy to meet me and spend some time together. I noticed that my generation in India gets older faster and perceive themselves as *"aged"* I could not relate to that part of life as we in the USA tend to value youth and make efforts to look young. However, I very much enjoyed relating to my cousins' children and even grandchildren.

The following year I donated $50,000 to Share and Care Foundation for its *"Educate to Graduate"* program, which helps empower women, to the *"Smile Train"* to correct cleft palate and cleft lip in children and to support "immunization program" in India.

I visited Jain temples in *Palitana,* a pilgrimage site for Jains. *Palitana* has been recognized as the first "Vegetarian" city in the world. I experienced the strength and power of faith, rituals and worship. These temples are widely visited by tourists from all over the world especially Jains. The main temple is over 1000 years old. I met several Caucasian non-Jains who had climbed 3600 steps of *Palitana Mountain* to see the beauty of the idols of *twenty-four Jain Tirthankara* (those who have reached Nirvana). This tour had offered me an opportunity to spend time with my two cousins, Manju and Pradip. We talked about our childhood, our aging parents in their eighties and our growing up years. We talked about our married life, our grown up children and gracefully graying phase of our lives.

I visited the most beautiful manmade city called *Lavassa,*

with my friend Amta and her family. It is located on a natural lake surrounded by *Sayadhari Mountains* in Maharashtra, a state where the thriving, vibrant city Mumbai is located. The breeze was pleasant. There was chill in the air and palpable warmth in our hearts. Lavassa is planned to be a model city located about four hours away from Mumbai.

I travel to India to visit all the charitable organizations where I donate money from the United States. Some of these visits have left lasting memories in my heart. I visited *Kutch* where children who were orphaned at the time of devastating earthquake are educated. This was my educational mission. I attended a class with seventh grade children, both boys and girls. The classroom was large and it had a large window which did not have window shades. The sunlight coming through the window had made the room hot. I noticed that all the boys were sitting in the part of the classroom where there was shade and all the girls were sitting in the sunny part of the classroom. I questioned all the boys why they were sitting together in one corner of the room. They promptly responded that the room was cooler in the shaded area. The girls responded that they usually sit after the boys have taken their seats. I asked the boys as to what happens if they sit in the sun. Once again they said with confidence that they would get dark (tanned). I asked the boys "who would you like to marry, dark or light colored women when you grow up?" Without hesitation they answered "Light colored girls." I observed that the preference for light colored skin was communicated without hesitation and that was a cultural phenomenon and not an individual's preference. However, they did not care that the girls they would like to marry (although not the same classmates) were getting tanned as they always sat in the sunny corners of the classroom. I presented this learning experience to the teachers and the principle of the school. Teachers stated that my observation was also replicated in their classrooms. I suggested if I could donate window shades in all classrooms and they happily accepted and implemented my suggestion. I learned from this episode that going in person to such places can be highly gratifying and an American dollar goes a long way here.

I visited *Raigadh* in Maharashtra and its surrounding villages. Through *Aarti foundation*. I have sponsored seventeen toilets to be installed in one village where there are fifty households and one hundred and fifty people live there. Through *Swadesh Foundation* the village has received running water in each house. My trip inspired me to sponsor four model villages where water, sanitation, medical and educational facilities will be available. It is my personal goal to empower the rural areas to reverse the current exodus of rural people to the cities looking for work.

I have visited *Hyderabad* where old city preserved from the time of Nizam rulers meets the new city which is the Silicon Valley of India. This city is also well known for its L.T. Prasad eye hospital. We saw the building from outside but our son, Viral, had an opportunity to work in this hospital for a month and receive unparalleled surgical experiences. I know he was grateful for this. Through *Hope Abides*, a US based charity; I sponsored three orphan boys' education to complete high school.

Any trip to India is never complete without shopping for ethnic clothes for children and grandchildren and dry snacks and sweets for everyone at home. Every place in India is well known for a local super-specialty food item that they are famous for. Tourists buy them as gifts as the family and friends wait back home to taste them. I have bought biscuits from Hyderabad, bhel with pomegranate from Palitana, gathia from Bhavnagar, adadia and penda from Rajkot, chikki from Lonavala, Khajala from Porbandar and so on. Our family and friends are always so happy when we come back with gifts from India.

The following year we flew from Mumbai to *Dehradun* and travelled by car from *Dehradun to Haridwar*. Our first stop was at

"*Ganga Aarti.*" Ganga Aarti means prayer to the River Ganges. Ganga is the holy river in India. It is worshipped as a goddess since it provides life in the form of water to India. Ganga Aarti occurs at Sunset each day on the bank of the river Ganges. There are a number of stories about Ganges emerging from the head of "*Lord Shiva*" in the Himalayas and meeting the land at this particular site. It is therefore romanticized. In Hinduism "*The Trimurti is a concept in which the cosmic functions of creation, maintenance and destruction or transformation are personified. Lord Brahma is the creator, Lord Vishnu is the maintainer or preserver and Lord Shiva is the destroyer and transformer.*"

At this *Aarti*, attendees and the pundits sing the devotional songs that emotionally and gratefully praise the God for giving us the beauty and the bounty of nature. Ganges is indeed a magnanimous river, which has sustained the lives of millions of people. It is therefore considered sacred and fondly called as "Ganga Maiya" (Mother Ganga). Water is part of Mother Nature that sustains life!

I like to imagine that in the ancient past when people's mobility was limited, when only a Saintly person would leave the civilization to meditate in the Himalayas to learn about the meaning of life. I also like to explain to myself, that the amazingly mighty Himalayas must have been perceived by these saints as nothing but *lord Shiva* and the magnanimous Ganges that emerges from the Himalayas as coming down from the head of Shiva. Every corner in this area, the faithful believers have built a temple of Shiva and lovingly addressed him as "*Bhole Nath*," a giving and non-critical Lord that destroys and transforms to keep the continuity of life.

The entire area of Uttarakhand has some tributaries of Ganges flowing through it. These tributaries flourish the farms and enrich the livelihood of this land. It has led to mythological, culturally based and spiritually enlightening stories around Ganga, which makes Ganga Aarti even more meaningful.

Here, we met several Caucasians from Europe and America at this site. They had included *Ganga Aarti* in their tour of India. Talking to them I was even more convinced that the ambience of *Ganga Aarti* had brought out the best in all who attended it. They were excited.

Trips to India can be physically and emotionally overwhelming but they are certainly inspiring and fulfilling spiritually. I have not only limited my trips to meeting families and friends but I have met a wide variety of people, rich and poor and had meaningful conversations, learned life lessons from them and shared mine with them. During earlier trips to India I felt an empty feeling when I returned back to my home in New York. India was my first home, my childhood paradise. But as I have grown older, and my grandparental generation has passed and some siblings have also moved on, it is hard to say whether it is the people or place or both that keeps me going back to India. The warmth of the people certainly nurtures me spiritually. But, if I really had to pin it down, India is my home. Nationality knows no boundaries. I am American, I am Indian, and I am both. I am an American of Indian origin. Once a young man in his 20s asked, "Where are you from?" I replied I am from New York. I waited for the next question. "But where are you originally from"? I replied, "I was born in India and I have lived in the USA for 47 years". I asked him his own question that he had asked me. "Where are you from?" With great astonishment he replied "I am from here". I asked him "How long have you lived here?" He paused and then with a smile of gratitude he said "You taught me something; the correct question would be where you were born"

As Swami Vivekananda has said, *"Happiness, we see, is what everyone is seeking for, but the majority seeks it in things which are evanescent and not real. No happiness was ever found in the senses or in the enjoyment of senses. Happiness is only found in the spirit."* Pleasures are not found in material things, they are found in the soul's wholeness.

I will continue to travel to India as long as I am physically able to do so. There are many more places I want to visit and experience the infinite joy and infinite bliss. But again, it is home, and I am in a state of bliss when I am there.

Auspicious Ganges river Aarti, Haridwar, India

Nalini and Sheetal in Rajkot, India

Travels With Three Children

Though we quite often paid travel agencies for the service, I greatly enjoy organizing and planning tours for our adventures. It is almost like traveling twice: I research the places we would enjoy visiting and then efficiently map out the route. This was the time when there was no internet. It's like a visualizing before and after with anticipations, building of imagined images climaxing upon the reveal of the actual thing. Sometimes places look as they appear, but I find that cameras, although great for memories, do not have the power to accurately convey a place's feel. Good photographers can come close to a memory, even feeling, but the actual is left for the mind and one's perception if they are lucky enough to remember. *William Faulkner* said that *"memory believes before knowing remembers."* But what you remember becomes you. What I'm saying is that through the process of planning the trip imagination expands---real expansion is not comparing the visceral before and after; it is the divine touch that forces you to feel the difference.

Anyway, after having done this I would find a travel agent who specializes in that part of the world where we want to explore. I do not have a back packer personality, it made me too anxious not to know the plan and be taken up by surprise. I guess having a type A personality, I take practical approaches to everything, especially methodical planning. Unlike me, Viren loves to do things spontaneously. However, he does not enjoy the researching part of traveling; he prefers to "just go". When the infrastructure of the tour was planned, I worked on the details and tried to jam-packed things to do which sometimes became over whelming and exhausting. I learned from such experiences to plan based on the level of stamina we all had and prioritize the places we could visit on each day. Birds eye view of different countries and cultures appealed to us since we did not take travel vacations to rest and relax. After each of our trips, we were refreshed with new experiences although, physically exhausted. Our travels did not include lying on the beach for all day long or doing sporty activities like many American friends I know tend to typically do. We also did not spend too much time in finding five stars restaurants because most of them did not offer good vegetarian food. We enjoyed eating food from different cultures and even learned how to prepare some dishes. Indian, Mexican and Italian and Mediterranean restaurants were usually able to meet our needs. I had learned from Julia, the wife of my uncle Jay, who taught me to say *"No Pesce, No Carne,"* meaning, *"No fish, No meat"*, while traveling in European countries. Still, in some restaurants, especially big and famous ones, the server did not take time to understand and explain to the chef in the kitchen what our needs were. I would then explain that we are vegetarians, pause while making full eye contact with the server. Then go on and say, that means we cannot eat meat, fish, chicken, pork and eggs. Very frequently we received a stunned face looking at us with an expression, "Then what do you eat?" Those were also the days when not too many people were vegetarians like us and the natives were not used to our food preferences. The word "Vegan" was not yet in the dictionary. We were usually offered a salad and bread which was not satisfying. We also had good experiences of eating in smaller local joints where people took time to make special food with fresh ingredients that appealed to our taste buds. Therefore, while traveling we did not have to make reservations in fancy restaurants. We also did not drink alcoholic drinks, and because of that, our meals were quite inexpensive. So while traveling we were soaked in the culture as long as our palates were satisfied eating healthy spicy vegetarian food.

We had taken several short trips with our children within the US. These were the sites where children enjoyed swimming, going to amusement parks and going on rides, and had many playing opportunities. We have three children; Manisha being the oldest daughter, Kapila, our middle daughter and the youngest is our son Viral. He is eight years younger than Manisha. As they were growing up their interests were changing but not at the same pace, obviously, because of the age difference. We wanted to take longer family vacations to faraway lands for sightseeing purposes and to see the world, and give this expansive worldview to our children. Like we knew, they needed to know that where they live is not the only place in the world, and in fact, if they look hard enough they just might find a differently vibrant world that has been all along. We had no idea if we will be able to enjoy these expensive trips since each one had different expectations. Whatever, we went for it.

Our first trip was to *Hawaii*. Viral was only four years old, and after a long flight we arrived in the *island of Oahu* late in the evening. A villa was reserved for us but the first step was to find our pre-reserved rental car. When we arrived at the rental car place we were told that the large car we had reserved was not available. We needed space so that all three children can spread out. Children saw a big van sitting there in the parking lot. They said out loud, *"we can take that big van!"* The man in the office was amused and said, *"well, then you can have it at the same rate as you had reserved your smaller car."* That's the island spirit. We had never driven a large van but it was fun and we stretched out, sang songs and played games. The children enjoyed swimming in the beach as well as in the pool. We then went to the *island of Kauai*. Our villa had the kitchen facing the mountains and the living room facing the ocean, comprehensive and expansive. Before we could even bring in the luggage, Viral came running out of the van and fell on his face, and as I looked at him and he looked at me, blood started rushing down his face. Two of his sisters began to provide nursing care. We were gratified to see how Manisha had become the big care giver and Kapila her assistant. They bonded while providing first aid to their little brother. We went to see the beautiful gardens where in one place there was a natural dripping of water. The legend went: *whoever makes a wish under the dripping water, their wish would come true.* I made a wish that our family of five would take many international trips together.

That year I also planned a two-week trip to south India where we travelled in an air-conditioned car. We travelled from *Goa to Madras (Chinnai) to Bangalore to Mysore to Ooty and finally to Kanya Kumari, the southernmost tip of India.* We enjoyed the sunset near the ashram of Swami Vivekanand in Kanya Kumari. We saw temples, beaches, museums, botanical gardens and the zoo. Children were fascinated to see that our hotels were actually royal palaces of the Maharajas, now converted into hotels. The richness of culture, warmth of people and variety of vegetarian food made all of us very happy. We bonded together and talked about our earlier life when we were growing up in India. The children, away from their daily routine, explored and learned about their parents' birthplace. Manisha, being the oldest understood what it was like for us when we immigrated to the US. That is a moment when you can look at your child like an adult—when they look at you like one and all of a sudden, with wide eyes, and *understand.*

The following year we took a bird's eye view of Europe tour. Though I can talk about how we went on a bus for two days in all these beautiful European cities, what really impressed us was that our children were able to note differences among people from one country to the other although they were all Caucasians. Manisha had one school friend whose parents had immigrated to the US from Switzerland and another one from France. These subtle differences in culture became real to her when we travelled through these countries. We realized that our children were getting older and independent. Even Viral at the age of eight managed his luggage and started to take care of his needs. Kapila has always learned and grasped new things beyond her age because she listened to Manisha's stories intently and processed new information rapidly.

We realized that Manisha was approaching end of high school. We had more travels in mind but the time was short. Regardless, we turned our focus to the orient, the great east, Asia. This tour started from *San Francisco to Bangkok*. Our flight from New York to San Francisco was delayed and our scheduled flight to Bangkok had already taken off. Since we had reserved each of the hotels and planned out sightseeing, on a tight schedule, this delay was frustrating. We tried to get on another flight but there were no seats in the economy class. However, there was one flight to Bangkok which had only five seats unoccupied in the business class. The airline staff was sad to see a family of five stranded. She got her manager and gave us all a seat in business class. We had never traveled in the business class before. All three children were thrilled when they began to receive their own travel bag and other goodies from the flight crew. This lovely start was more than what we had expected. It was surely a turn of the tides, and an excellent start. We slept through the night and arrived in Bangkok refreshed. We continued on to *Hong Kong, Singapore, Tokyo, Kyoto and Hakone in Japan*. Viren carried his video camera and I carried my still camera. All our memories were captured during these trips. However, one experience in *Hakone* lasted. We got on a Cable car sky ride to travel from one mountain to the other. We were all five in the same cable car. It was big and comfortable. While we were enjoying the beautiful mountains, deep valley and the forests, we heard someone talk in Japanese through the radio communication in the cable car. We looked at each other because none of us knew what was being said. Our cable car was between the two mountains from where we could see nothing but the sky, the valley and the mountains. Someone noticed that our cable car was swinging, meaning it was very windy outside. The radio communication continued but we had no idea what was going on. After a few serious moments, one of our children said that we should all pray because there was something wrong and we were in danger. Viral was known to be the family clown. He said that if we pray to Hindu God, in Japan no one will understand our prayers. Kapila said we should pray to the Shinto God. She remembered that we had visited Shinto temples in Kyoto. Manisha said we should pray to the Buddhist God because most Japanese people prayed to Buddha. By now our fear for safety had taken a turn. We were giggling trying to find the right God who could take us to our destination. Viren noticed that our cable car was moving not just swinging. The Japanese narration was continuing too. I noticed that the cable car from the opposite side had just about passed us, meaning we were certainly moving. Sure enough, we arrived on the other side of the mountain. As we got off the cable car we saw a crew of journalist with cameramen trying to interview us. Manisha being the most mature of the children took a lead and told them that we did not understand Japanese. One of the journalists spoke English. He told us that there was a wind storm which had halted the cable cars for half an hour. They wanted us to tell them about our experience. We all cracked up because we could not figure out which one of the Gods we were praying to have saved us. I think they appreciated it, too.

Manisha was going to college. Our household shrunk and we could not imagine taking tours as a family of five any more. The tour experience would be incomplete without her. But Manisha was very willing to accompany us to a tour of North India when she had the time. Our Children saw a vast difference in the cultures of

North and South India. We went to see the *Taj Mahal* and took most beautiful pictures. Those days, in 1992, we could not see the pictures right away after taking them because they were not digital. After returning back home our pictures were developed. We were hysterical to see that many of those pictures were double exposed and they looked ridiculously funny. Well, well, we said *"We have to visit again to take better pictures."*

The following year, in 1993, we took a tour of *Alaska*. By now, children chose where to visit and Alaska was their choice. It was not well travelled by tourists at that time. I loved to read, study each place and planned out a tour of Alaska where we would use every means of transportation. We arrived in *Anchorage*. It was warm during day time and cold at nights. Wearing layers of clothes was necessary. We even found an Indian restaurant where we enjoyed vegetarian food. In our rental car we travelled to *Valdez* where Exxon oil spill had occurred. We took an overnight ship that could carry our car with us and arrived at *Kodiak Island*. We saw a number of fishermen who were immigrants of Filipino origin. Next day the ship brought us back to Anchorage. Our next destination was through all glassed train to the *Danali Park*. This was an amazing experience. All of us loved natural beauty. In Danali Park we went horse-back riding to tour the park. From Danali Park our next destination was *Fairbanks* where on the steam boat which sailed along the coast giving us beautiful view of the coastal villages. From Fairbanks we took a small plane to the top of the world, *"Barrows"* which is located at the Arctic Circle. Very few tour companies took tourists to Barrows. We had planned to watch the midnight sun. There was only one hotel with all glass windows from ceiling to the floors where we stayed overnight. There was one Mexican restaurant where we ate vegetarian spicy Mexican food we love. The owner told us that everything we ate was flown to Barrows because nothing grew there.

We met some local Native Indians who were preparing for

a festival called *"Whaling."* We were curious to know about the celebration. We did know that each year the young local men would go out to the ocean to hunt a whale. If they succeed in killing the whale, this whale would provide the food for the local people throughout the year. We figured that they were celebrating the courage of young people who had successfully hunted the whale. But we were wrong. It was fascinating to hear that they were celebrating the life of the whale because she had given up her life for the survival of the people. It was truly a spiritual way of looking at life and survival, although in reality, they slaughtered a whale to survive.

The most exciting thing was to watch the midnight sun as that happens in the summer. The sun never sets. We watched sun set from one side of the Arctic Ocean and sunrise from the other side. This was the most amazing experience which none of us could ever forget. All three children felt that these family travels had made them knowledgeable about the world and many cultures that we had visited. We discussed that happiness we had experienced is what everyone is seeking for but the majority seeks it in things which are not permanent. We had found happiness in the spirit of human beings and ever changing natural beauty. We talked about the spirit of the native people of Alaska. When one of our children asked a native about how they tolerated the cold weather year round in Barrows, she replied *"Weather, is never bad, it is only intolerable when people wear inappropriate clothing,"* She made us speechless. There was some truth in how she looked at nature and ways in which people can enjoy what nature offers.

When Kapila graduated from Law school and Viral graduated from college it was their desire to celebrate their graduations on a family tour. Manisha was in Medical school and could not join us. We went on a cruise to *Galapagos Islands.* These islands have no humans that live there—that is probably why they are so pristine. We visited the islands every day from our cruise ship. It was here that Darwin had developed his theory of evolution and wrote *The Voyage on the Beagle*. Sea lions sun bathed on the beach. They are not afraid of humans. Viral went swimming, came back and said that he swam with the sea lions next to him. They were neither afraid of humans nor needed to attack them. There was a spiritual connectedness around us.

Time flew by and children grew up, went to college and professional schools, got married and now have children of their own. One thing they have carried with them is the importance of family travels. Travels bonded us, matured us and made us wise. We watched our children change, mature, and become care givers to each other and to us. Now as adults, Manisha and Kapila have continued to travel with their spouses and children domestically as well as internationally and pass on this travel experience. Viral and his wife Rupa continue to take vacations to exotic places such as Island of Bora Bora and to experience the safari of South Africa. They have invited us to join them on some of their travels. Now our children are the planners of the trips.

Viral and Kapila at the Taj Mahal, Agra, India

Viral and Nalini at Ram Baugh Palace, Jaipur, Rajasthan, India

Viral, Kapila, Nalini and Viren at London
Bridge, London, England, Europe.

Kapila, Nalini and Manisha in Kimono outfit, Tokyo, Japan

Kapila, Viren, Nalini, Viral, Manisha in Kyoto, Japan

Manisha, Nalini and Ishani, three generational
women at Hilton Head, South Carolina, USA

Travelling With Friends

Our youngest, son, Viral had matriculated in University of Pennsylvania, and—finally as we say here—we had an empty nest. Although on one hand we were very happy that we had raised three wonderful children who had excelled in schools, received highest awards from teachers and recognized academic and personal excellence, we missed celebrating their daily achievements, naughty laughter, teasing each other and simply their presence on a daily basis. All three of them had received highest award from their high school for not only academic accomplishment but also for character integrity. The superintendent of the High School told me on the day of the final award night when Viral was graduating, that we were the only parents in the history of our school, who had all three children recognized by their high school teachers with such awards. Needless to say, we were proud of their accomplishments and integrity with which they were moving on to the next phase of life. Now there was a void. Whatever day to day role we had played in their lives was over. They were now independent and we admired their ability to be independent and responsible normal adults. As parents we knew that we had to move on with our lives and continue to be there when they needed us. We had to return back to our lives as it was before we had children. That time seemed far, far away, but we needed to reconnect as spouses and not just mommy and daddy. Some couples wait until their children leave the house to get divorced, we decided to strengthen the relationship when it was just us.

Viren and I took several trips with Indian friends who we had known for minimum of ten to a maximum of thirty-five years. Some of these tours included larger groups of forty people, mostly couples, while some of these tours were with smaller groups ranging from six to twelve people. Most of our friends are in the same age group as us, had similar immigration history and with similar interests in travelling. This made the connection easy. It was at that time that we decided to join our friends on a tour of *China*. The travel agent had arranged for us to have vegetarian Indian food every day for dinner. We arrived in *Beijing*, which was our first stop, but I had my eyes set on the Great Wall. We walked up to ride the cable car from the top of the preserved section of the Great Wall of China. As our turn came to jump in the cable car I noticed a big sign which stated that *"This car was used by President Clinton when he visited China."* It was a nostalgic feeling to know that we were riding the same cable car as our former president. We enjoyed the beautiful sweeping views of the surrounding forests and countryside around the wall. After experiencing this true wonder of the world, we walked down the steps. The vendors were selling their beautiful figurines, Jade statues of Buddha and many more all along the path. I picked up a statue of Jade Buddha and inquired about its price. The lady vendor did not speak any English but quickly pulled out a small sticky note pad and wrote the price in dollars. Seeing me somewhat confused to see its price in dollars, the vendor said "only a plastic card, Madame". I had to laugh that she called the credit card as insignificant as just a plastic card. I said "How much in Yen?" She looked at me with disgust. She said "dollar, dollar," meaning the only currency she would accept.

We spent half a day in Tiananmen Square, explored the Imperial grandeur of the Forbidden City and its history. China's communist environment was somewhat unsettling for us. One of our friends went as far as to feel that we should not be talking about their communist history and our discomfort in public. He said that *"They are watching everyone here."*

Our visit to Xian, a modern city cloaked in over 3000 years of history was most fascinating. Once it was the last stop on the Great Silk Road. Xian appealed to me as a melting pot of Chinese culture with influences from Middle Eastern and other Asian cultures. We visited the excavation site of the Terra Cotta Warriors and Horses; the life size army created during Qin Dynasty to protect China's first emperor in his afterlife. I began to think about the fear and insecurity these very powerful people must have felt about their death and after life, which may have led them to make preparation to protect themselves in the next life while they were still alive. The craftsmanship of each of the soldiers and the horses was remarkable. At the entrance of this excavation site sat an elderly man who seemed to know all about the excavation and the history of the place. Tourists were not allowed to take pictures or movies. Some things are better left for memories.

Every day our tour guide would take us to a large building where we ate Chinese lunch on the main floor. The waitresses did not communicate in English but swiftly dropped food plates on the lazy Susan on our table. We could not get additional supply of any item that we cherished because our request was met with a smile but no action. They had no interest in knowing about our needs. This was the most traumatic as well as amusing experience. That building was also a shopping mall. On each floor there were displays of arts, crafts, carpets and beautiful things to buy as souvenirs. I was amazed to watch the artists on premise working on their individual pieces. Chinese people impressed me as very hard working, smart and determined to do whatever they set their minds on. One example has stayed with me for all these years. We showed interest in a hand woven silk wall carpet piece which was three feet by four feet in size. The shop quoted us its price to be $700. We walked away because it was too expensive for our budget. The shop sent its sales men wherever we went. It was amazing to see them show up every time our bus stopped for sightseeing. When we saw their determination to sell this carpet piece, Viren said that he had expected to buy two pieces for $500. He thought that this ridiculous offer would get them so annoyed that they will leave us alone. We finally reached our hotel. Seated on the sofa in the lobby, we were surprised to see that the salesman was waiting for us to arrive. They agreed to sell these two carpet pieces for $500. We were delighted to buy them. We have these two beautiful pieces hanging on our wall in the entrance of our bedroom reminding us of this beautiful tour of China and our encounters with the Chinese people. However, eating Chinese food for every lunch for fifteen days was certainly not a pleasurable experience. On the last day, our group declared a strong protest against having Chinese food for lunch. We had seen a "Pizza Hut" on our way during our sightseeing. We protested "pizza or no lunch." The local guide finally gave in and we were all delighted to eat our favorite pizza from Pizza Hut.

This travel gave us time and relaxation to reflect on our life ahead. We returned home with an inner sense of peace. Joy had returned back to our spirit. It was visible to our children because they said *"You did not call or anything during these fifteen days."* They were not happy. There was no easy availability of internet or phone calls at that time. They were worried but we realized we were lost in our own world.

Our next tour with friends was to *Russia, Scandinavian countries (Denmark, Norway, Sweden), and Iceland.* We were a smaller group this time. In Russia we concentrated on visiting *Moscow and St. Petersburg.* We explored captivating architectural and cultural treasures on this journey. This fascinating region with picturesque medieval towns, opulent palaces and cathedrals took our breaths away. The State Hermitage Museum in St Petersburg and the glories of *Peterhof, the Russian Versailles* was truly awe inspiring. Moscow's art museums and a tour of the Kremlin are memorable, not that you would want to gallivant around the Kremlin nowadays. We talked to the young Russians who were enjoying the newly acquired freedom while the older generation Russians were pessimistic about freedom. They said that it is only a question of time when Russia will return back to communist ideology. Friends tell me that the older people in former Soviet countries have a mythical nostalgia about the "good old days," and that we will return to the Soviet era very, very soon. It is a little bit like when you hear in the Southern United States, *"the South will rise again!"*

Australia and New Zealand: We were on our way to another continent with a group of friends again. This tour showed us the natural marvels as well as those made by humankind. Some places have a nice balance of the two forms of creation. This trip highlighted the importance. We arrived in Sydney and took a walking tour of the town. It was very interesting to learn that this new continent Australia was built by English prisoners and debtors who were sent off to this far away land. The most amazing thing was that their crimes that imprisoned them were close to misdemeanors as we would call them today. Sydney's Opera House was recognized by UNESCO in 2007 as a great architectural work of 20th century. As we were walking around this magnanimous structure, we learned that an opera was on in the evening at the Sydney's Opera House. We had not reserved tickets ahead of time; however, we did have a hope that we may find some tickets. We were ten friends on this tour. I took courage to ask the ticket booth if we could get ten tickets for the show. We wanted to sit together if possible. She smirked and said that it was house full. However, since we were visiting for just two days, she said there were ten tickets on the side of the stage. At this point I was prepared to take anything that was available. My friends also agreed to sit on the side. We arrived for the show in the evening and got seated. We sat so close to the stage; you could feel the wind from the singing.

On our bus tour further we visited family owned sheep farms, bountiful vineyards and arrived at the *Great Barrier Reef.* We took the catamaran cruise out to the greatest barrier reef to watch the underwater memorable sea life. Viren snorkeled for the first time in his life. We visited Sydney's *Featherdale Wildlife Park* to visit some of the Australia's native animals that thrive in the natural bush setting. We watched Koalas eating eucalyptus leaves. I took several pictures with the cuddly koalas, friendly kangaroos and wallabies. We watched the Aboriginal art and their dancing. These natives told us stories about Australia's earliest days. The most memorable trip was to the charming *Melbourne.* There was a distinctive European feeling with Victorian era charm here. We visited its beach where tourists come to watch the *Penguins' March.* At sunset we all sat on the bleachers. We watched penguins swim ashore few at a time and hanged out there until the entire community of penguins that lived on that beach arrived. Then they organized themselves in a row with the head of the team leading the way. I will never forget these penguins' behaviors. I wish we humans can learn from these animals how to live in harmony. They live under the covered bridge that took us to the beach. This experience wetted my interest to visit these penguins in Antarctica.

We flew to *Wellington, New Zealand's waterfront capital.* We learned about the pacific and Maori cultures. We cruised the Milford Sound and watched New Zealand's breath taking scenery. The naturalist on board showed us its cliffs and glacier-hewn inlets. Our journey continued on to the beautiful south island landscapes to *Queenstown.* It is no surprise that they filmed *Lord of the Rings* here.

As usual, we looked for some Indian food for dinner. We learned that there were Indian immigrants to Australia and New

Zealand. We guessed that there must be some Indian restaurants. Sure enough, we found one. The owner was so delighted that a group of us, all of Indian origin living in America were going to dine in his restaurant that night. He gathered a group of musicians who sang *Hindi* songs and played instrumental music.

There is a definite sense of familiarity and intimacy that people feel when they run into each other when traveling. Travels bring strangers together, and often those strangers become friends. Travels also bring a special charm of intimacy when they encounter familiar people, like the man in Michigan who ran to us with open arms saying *"My countrymen, you are here"*

Africa: We were three couples who decided to travel to East and South Africa. Africa is a continent where wildlife of all size and color from the big five: buffalo, elephant, leopard, lion and rhinoceros, herds of deer, zebra, hyenas, leopards, cheetahs, hippos, jackals, and villagers, safari trackers, conservationists and tourists travel through game rich parks every day. Although we have taken *Tanzania Safari*, we have yet not taken *Kenya safari*. We have traveled through *Serengeti, Maasai Mara, Arusha, and Ngorongoro crater.* The circle of life unfolds in front of your eyes on these safaris. Safari lovers return year after year. I met a few on our tour. We were just three very close couples traveling for the first time together.

We arrived in *Arusha.* The snow on *Kilimanjaro Mountains* was the first amazing site we saw from the airport as it was a clear bright day. Our next stop was *Ngoro Ngoro* conservation area. We were told by our tour guide that *Ngoro Ngoro Crater* was considered by many to have been Africa's original *"Garden of Eden".* Within this dormant volcano there is inspiring continuous animal migration. It was a great location for spotting wildlife. Our hotel was located on the rim of the dormant volcano. It provided amazing views of the "Lost world" below us. Within the crater lie grasslands, forests and a salt water lake. We took morning and evening game drives in our open four wheel drive jeep accompanied by a driver with sharp eyes always looking out to spot one of the wild animals. It is an amazing experience to observe these animals in their natural habitat. Our driver was alerted by other drivers that a lioness was spotted hiding on top of the crater which meant that she was preparing to catch her prey.

En route to *Serengeti,* we stopped at *Oldupai Gorge,* where the earliest man walked upright some 3.6 million years ago. We witnessed the vast landscapes and remarkable wildlife of *Serengeti National Park,* a UNESCO World Heritage site.

We visited a *Maasai village* where we were personally welcomed by a Maasai Mara elder who had several wives with whom he had several children. They all lived together in a large area. I enjoyed spending some time with the children who are intrigued by variety of tourists who visit them daily. We saw Maasai herdsman grazing their cattle alongside the zebras. The Maasai hunt lions. They have an eternal relationship with the beasts. But because of this, they are causing the populations to decrease. It is a very complicated conflict

Our tour included a visit to *Zanzibar,* which had attracted traders from India and the Middle East. It had become the key place where slave trade was highly profitable. Cloves, ivory, coffee, tea, and gold were all part of the trade. It had attracted traders from Europe, especially the British.

African cuisine for vegetarian diet included a number of options, which included some fusion between Indian and African food. Indian traders, businessman, teachers have settled in Africa, especially in Tanzania, Kenya, Zanzibar and Ethiopia for several years when India was one of the British Colonies. They may have also influenced the cuisines of East Africa.

South Africa: We arrived in *Cape Town* and then we drove along the cape peninsula to Cape Point where we saw sensational views of the *Cape of Good Hope.* Our next stop was at *Johannesburg,* the largest city of South Africa. We attended a presentation by a gemologist who told us about the history of Africa's diamonds, gold and other precious stones. We visited the *Soweto Township* where homes of *Nelson Mandela* and *Archbishop Desmond Tutu* are located. We visited the prison where Nelson Mandela was imprisoned. The most heart wrenching experience was at the *Apartheid Museum*. At the heart of this museum is the apartheid story, its rise and its fall. It is acknowledged as the pre-eminent museum in the world dealing with 20th century South Africa. The entrance to museum had a separate door for men and women. It made me feel that I was different, perhaps inferior. It gave me a unique South African experience. It was an emotional journey that took me through the experiences of people who were discriminated based on their race. This experience of visiting Apartheid Museum made me understand the story of *Mohandas Karamchand Gandhi* who had started to practice law in South Africa after receiving law degree in Britain. While traveling on a train with a higher class ticket he encountered a white man who summoned him to get off the train because he was not white. His suitcase was thrown out of the train and he had to get off. This experience led Gandhi to the fight for independence from the mighty British Empire. He took this experience further to India where struggle for independence began. We saw the statue of Gandhi with his suitcase on the ground at the site where he was summoned to get off the train in Johannesburg. It is indeed a proud moment to see the statue of *Mahatma Gandhi* in several continents of the world. We have seen it in New York, USA, Winnipeg, Canada, Chile, and South America.

Our emotionally charged tour ended at the *Victoria Falls in Zimbabwe*. We took a guided walk to the viewpoints to enjoy the falls and its surrounding rain forests. Victoria Falls is one of the Seven Wonders of the World. It offers a spectacular sight of awe inspiring beauty and grandeur on the Zambezi River.

Africa is a continent where resources abound. The beauty of nature is incredible, expansive, and constantly reminds me of where we come from, and where we will go.

South East Asia: This was a 13 days tour, which started and ended in Mumbai. Indians from India have migrated to various countries of Southeast Asia over at least 1000 years. Most of these Indians had emerged from south India and some had immigrated after the partisan of India and Pakistan.

Our first stop was in **Bali, Indonesia** which is a beautiful beach resort but beyond that the Balinese people have strong spiritual roots and their culture is very much alive. 90% of the population is Indian Hindus. Hindus from southern part of India had arrived in Bali in the 11th century. Their main religion is called *Agma Hindu Dharma* which although originally from India, it comprises of a unique blend of Hindu and Buddhist, Javanese and ancient indigenous belief system. It has evolved to an extent that it is very different from the Hinduism practiced in India today. The Balinese worship the *Hindu trinity Brahma, Vishnu and Shiva.* I was very impressed by these people who have preserved their religious values through rituals, names, characters, musical instruments, and dances. They brought *"Ramayana and Mahabharata,"* two Hindu scriptures with them when they arrived in Bali thousand years ago, and even today they present plays and musicals based on the stories from these scriptures. Most of their beautiful arts and crafts have been inspired by the stories from the Ramayana and the Mahabharata Hindu epics. We watched one play from Mahabharata, which described that there is an eternal fight between good and evil which is in all of us and it will always be there. But human efforts can get rid of the evil and good will prevail. People believe in Karma. The national language is Balinese. Children are taught *Balinese and Sanskrit (an ancient Indian language).* I had learnt Sanskrit as a second language in High school in India but could not communicate with them in

Sanskrit. Balinese people believe that good spirits dwell in the mountains. Most villages have three temples. 1. Temple of origin, facing the mountains, 2. Village temple found in the center of the village and 3. Temple aligned with the sea and dedicated to the spirits of the dead. We visited some of these temples on seaside and on mountains, which people visit twice a month. Everyone has a home temple for private worship.

Some of the people we talked to conveyed pride in having an Indian identity.

Since in Indonesia majority of the population is Muslim we were surprised to meet so many Hindus. The locals told us that Muslim majority was only in Jakarta which we did not visit.

Our second stop was *Kuala Lumpur in Malaysia*. Malaysian people were the first Indian people who came to Malaysia. British followed them and ruled the country until 1957. They consider *Mahatma Gandhi* as their first father of Independence. Natives speak Malay, English, Tamil and Chinese which are all languages taught in schools. Indians who emerged from south India have settled here. We met their descendants who were fifth generation of the earlier settlers. Malaysians believe in the spirit of optimism and self-assurance. When cultural, religious, or political conflicts arise they advocate going beyond tolerance and embracing acceptance and understanding of each other.

Kuala Lumpur is well known for its modern urban life with skyscrapers and its cosmopolitan population.

There is a temple, which has the idol of *Lord Murugan (Shiva)*. It is 140 feet tall and located in a cave called *Batu caves*. This statue is the tallest in the world. It is said that 400 years ago British discovered this temple in the mountain made of all lime stone. We climbed 272 steps to go inside the cave where there was an excavated temple.

We witnessed an annual Hindu religious function near this temple. It was amazing that over five generations of Malay people had preserved Hindu religious rituals. The locals said that the Hindus, Muslims, Chinese and Malay people live together peacefully in Malaysia.

We visited the twin towers which were built in 1990. This is the tallest structure in the East today and belonged to a businessman of Indian origin. Government of Malaysia bought these towers from him and gave them to *Petronas* Company. Therefore, they are called *Petronas towers*. They are made of glass and iron and there is a huge mall underneath. We visited a Chinese Buddhist temple, a bird park and a butterfly garden which is considered largest in the east. Our third stop was in *Siem Reap in Cambodia*. There are 293 temples in *Siem Reap*. *Angkor Wat* is the oldest temple visited by tourists from far and wide. History shows that Southeast Asia has been inhabited since the Neolithic era, but the seeds of Angkorian civilization were sown in the first century A.D. At the turn of the millennium, South East Asia was becoming a hub for commercial trading network. Indian and Chinese traders arrived in greater numbers exposing the indigenous people to their cultures. Indian culture took hold through the efforts of Hindu Brahmin priests. Hinduism and Buddhism spread over a period of several centuries. Angkor Wat is a temple constructed artistically as a massive three-tiered temple mountain dedicated to the Hindu God Vishnu. Although Angkor Wat was constructed to be a Hindu temple, it has also served as a Buddhist temple since Buddhism became Cambodia's dominant religion in the fourteenth century.

Viren took tons of pictures. He found an amazing site where he wanted me to sit with the back drop of Ankor wat temple. This site was on a hill. Right behind him was a slippery slope of the hill. We both were settled for this particular photo shoot. As he was focusing for an ideal picture, I saw him moving a step at a time backwards. At one point his feet slipped. He caught himself and regained his balance. If he had not caught himself, an inch further would have taken him down the hill. I stopped breathing with my eyes closed anticipating the most deadly event. To this day, thinking of this scenario I get goosebumps and night mares. Viren has always loved to take my pictures ever since we met. This was the epitome of him.

Our tour guide told us that in the capital city of Cambodia there are over 1000 Hindu temples, and four hours away from Siem Reap there is a river where 1000 heads of Hindu Gods have been found. The locals said that Hindus came first to Cambodia 700 years ago and Buddhists came 300 years ago. At present, Hinduism and Buddhism are combined and all Hindu Gods and Buddha are worshipped. Souls of ancestors were worshipped prior to that. Although currently, it is known to be a Buddhist country, in temples both Hindu and Buddhist rituals are conducted. Cambodians are very poor people and American dollar can really go a long way.

Our next stop was in *Ho Chi Minh (Saigon) in South Vietnam.* This is a modern democracy-loving place, which is under communist government. Although Vietnam War lasted here for over 10 years (1960-1975), people were not bitter. We learned that the war was along the coasts and along the borders of Cambodia, Laos and on the border of South and North Vietnam. South Vietnam wanted democracy while North wanted communism. The most memorable site was *Cu Chi tunnels* which are an immense network of connecting underground tunnels located in the Ho Chi Minh City, Vietnam. Our tour guide, at that time, was a six years old boy whose father was in the war and captured by North Vietnamese army. His mother was taking care of the soldiers and he was responsible for his three years old sister. He showed us the village scene with fruit bearing trees all over and the areas, which were destroyed by American bombings.

When Americans bombed this area, the farmers dug up a tunnel where they were able to hide. It was dug up with ordinary farming tools. This underground tunnel system is situated within

Cu Chi battlefield. It has several floors and several deviated alleys like a cobweb with its places for boarding, accommodation, and meeting rooms. Vietnamese people are small and they could squeeze through small openings of the tunnel. This underground tunnel system was very inspiring. It indicated the will and determination, wisdom and pride of Cu Chi people. They created a whole town with hospital etc. in the tunnel. When American soldiers learned about these tunnels they tried to go in but got trapped. The farmers had also created sharp piercing rods, which rotated and trapped the soldiers and many young inexperienced US soldiers died in this kind of guerrilla warfare. Our tour guide said that he felt very sad to see these very young US soldiers die such a treacherous death. This was a difficult day to remember the Vietnam War days. We had arrived in the US in 1970. Vietnam War news was on the front pages of the Newspapers. We were struggling to settle in the new land while the unpopular war was on.

We visited the war museum, which was very touching and made me sad. I realized that my American identity was so strongly established that it hurt to know that many of our young soldiers died here. We also visited the palace of the last king in 1975 when Saigon fell to communist North Vietnam. I reflected back on those earlier days because we were new immigrants in the USA at that time.

This was a critical time in the life of many Indian immigrants who had not taken Immigrant status nor taken citizenship for the fear of being drafted in the Vietnam War. We had yet not developed loyalty to the new country where we had just arrived. It hurt to remember those days of Vietnam War, an ugly chapter in American history.

Overall it was a moving experience. Our tour guide said that most Vietnamese after 50 years of war feel sad for those Vietnamese soldiers as well as for young inexperienced American soldiers who died.

We then arrived at our last stop in *Hanoi, North Vietnam.* Hanoi is a typical urban city with pollution, over population and Chinese influence since it is closer to China. It does not have large corporations and business sectors like what we saw in Saigon

From Hanoi we took an overnight cruise to *Halong Bay,* which is considered World Heritage site by UNESCO. We cruised for about an hour and found ourselves in the middle of thousand islands, each one without habitation but they have tall mountains. This was the most beautiful site ever. Since our visit to Vietnam was during the week of Vietnamese (Chinese) Lunar New Year we witnessed celebrations, lighting and decorations of streets and homes. People were visiting their parents and grandparents who live in the rural areas while young people work in the cities. The cruise boat had our group of fourteen people and a couple from Singapore. This kind of privacy made the cruise experience even more special.

We saw large floating villages on the coast of Vietnam as well as in Cambodia.

These villages are self-sufficient. They have a school, a hospital, and market for produce. People from these floating villages take small boats and sail out to sell their arts, crafts and their produce. Amazingly, little kids learn their marketing skills by accompanying their parent or older sibling in these boats. They did not wear any seat belts nor did they have any floats.

Myanmar: It was known as Burma during 60 years of British rule and 3 years of Japanese rule. *Bagan,* an ancient city known for its thousand years old temples, Pagodas and Stupas was our first stop in Myanmar. These sites have been declared as world heritage sites. 80% of the population of Myanmar is Buddhist and 20% Christians, Hindus and Moslems

Myanmar became independent from British rule in 1948, after India became independent in 1947. From early sixties onwards it was under military rule which did not allow tourist to come in for more than 7 days. The country was not exposed to the world through media, journalism etc.

In 2012, the New Democratic Party took over and tourism has flourished in last five years. We had a Buddhist tour guide called Kok which was a name he had taken to make it easy for his guests to address him. He said that all Buddhist men are required to become a monk for 7 days twice in their lives; once at age 8 and for the second time at age 18. Becoming a monk includes shaving off the head, wearing the robe; (color varies from those who live in Burma vs. other Buddhist countries), asking for food donations and learning scriptures in *Sanskrit and Pali* languages. The monks eat some breakfast and only one meal at 12.00 noon. Kok lived the life of a monk twice in his life. He remembered those weeks as a good experience, which trained him to live a simple good life using Buddhist principles

Kok was an ambitious smart guy who aspired to be upwardly mobile while staying within Bagan. He had hopes that his country will flourish someday.

When we left Bagan, I wanted to give Kok a small token of appreciation. I gave him my hat, which I had bought in Ecuador, South America. He wore it right away and appreciated its shape and the words Ecuador written on it. He loved the strings which kept its shape. Kok wanted to visit the world but for now he said "This hat will remind me that someday I can visit Ecuador, South America" He was a grateful human being, proud of his country and proud to welcome tourists in his country. He took us to watch sunset from the rooftop of a temple. This beautiful view included a panoramic view of the many temples and pagodas we visited. Kok was a wonderful photographer as well. He quickly figured out that I captured scenes of nature in my iPhone camera and he captured our photos in the backdrop of the nature

Knowing that we were vegetarians, Kok took us to an all vegetarian restaurant where we had delicious local food items. I saw that the waiters wore a T-shirt with print saying, "*Be kind to animals.*" I bought one such T shirt to remind me of this restaurant in Bagan.

Kok also took us on a walk to see a typical village where women did their household work; children were in school with very few resources.

I was very touched to see older children painted cards that tourists buy as souvenirs. These were handmade and they sold them. It was heartwarming to see that these children were earning while using their creativity. Kok wanted us to taste freshly fried vegetable fritters sold by a woman who ran this as her business. She sat in an open area outside her house, had a few benches for guests to sit and enjoy her freshly fried fritters. Neighbors would come and buy them from her. Kok assured us that these freshly fried fritters were safe to eat and he was right. It felt good for a change to step out of the tourists' shoes and to do what the locals did.

Our next city to visit was *Mandalay*. Once again we visited a number of Pagodas but the most memorable one was *Mahamuni Pagoda*, where various positions of Buddha statues provide an amazing feeling of peace. From the top of this temple we watched the sunset. We found that each pagoda was very unique in its architecture, paintings and positions of Buddha. We even visited a temple, which had fasting Buddha statue. The other amazing thing was that these Buddha statues are huge. We could watch that peaceful site from the roads as well. Next day we met our new tour guide. *Mu Mu* was a Muslim woman who told us that her great grandfather came to Burma from an area in India, which would now fall in *Bangla Desh*. She described three generations in her family who were married to Burmese spouses. She quickly felt that we were part of her "kind" of people and enjoyed giving us fine details of the places we visited. She gave us a special tour of a resort town where British spent their summers. It was heartwarming to see a Hindu temple in this town and eat in an Indian restaurant located on a river. I watched a woman wash her clothes on the bank of the river while her two sons played in the water. Such peaceful country sites attracted me.

Our next stop was Inle Lake. This river has a floating village. We traveled up and down the river in a motorboat for several hours. Our tour guide was Su Su. She took us to a floating restaurant, which served very tasty vegetarian rice dishes. We visited several local factories that made wood carved objects, lacquer ware, silk products and showed us the process of how the final product was made.

The most interesting of all was the making of string from lotus leaves. The lady who was making the string took one and tied it around our wrists. This gesture had a special meaning for me because Hindus celebrate a festival day named *"Raksha bandhan"* when a sister ties a string around the wrist of her brother. It is a symbol of protection. In old days when the warriors went to the war this string was tied as a gesture of well wishes to protect the warrior. I was reminded of the Croatian red tie which had similar significance. Our hotel was also floating on the river. Greenery and land scaled grounds in the heart of this scenic place was memorable.

Our last stop was in Yangon, known as Rangoon in the past. Like any other metropolis, it has diverse population that has created their own ghettos, which suffice their ethnic needs. We visited China town, South Asian town as well as local vendors sitting on the side walk preparing freshly made local delicacies. Each vendor had a few stools around them where people sat, got served hot food while they talked. There is less of a fear of catching infections from the food they ate. Although many items they freshly prepared and sold were vegetarian, we were afraid to indulge, as our American stomachs would react immediately. I was touched to watch the group sitting on those stools surrounding the vendor, talking and watching her prepare fresh street food that everyone enjoyed. We obviously could not do the same because during all our travels, we have to be vigilant in eating as any sickness would destroy the pleasure of travels

Our travel to Myanmar was very unique. The people are poor but incredibly honest, warm and caring. They continue to maintain discipline that they had to learn during military rule.

Travels teach us so much about life in various parts of the world. Many struggle to survive and it inspires me to see their perseverance to live. Creativity is the mother of inventions and cannot be better experienced than in these parts of the world.

Viren and Nalini in the same Cable car where President Clinton sat a year earlier to view the Great Wall of China, Beijing, China

Viren and Nalini in the museum where Terracotta Army of the first emperor of China, Qin Shi Huang located in Shaanxi, China

Chinese artist demonstrating his artwork to Nalini in Beijing, China

Butterfly Garden in New Zealand

Viren and Nalini in St. Petersburgh, Russia

140 feet tall idol of Lord Murugan (Shiva, Hindu God) in Batu Caves, Kuala Lumpur, Malaysia

Marble Statues of standing and sitting Buddha in South Vietnam

Traveling with Organized Tours

T our companies like *Globus* appealed to us as it offered affordable tours that attracted travelers from all parts of the world. We met travel companions from the United States, Australia, New Zealand, and Canada. And through this tour group, we travelled to *Western Europe, Eastern Europe, South America, Israel, Palestine, Spain, Portugal and Morocco, and Canadian Rockies.* I learned to pick the tour which would meet our desire to visit a lot of places and offer us a good sense of how people in other parts of the world live, our counterparts. To tour the way we want, we needed a guide who would go the extra mile, talk about everything under the sun, and show us the insider's view. Choosing a guide was not in our control.

As of writing this book we have only taken two fantastic tours namely "Polar Bear Excursion" and "A week in Spain" with *Tauck* tour company. Although a little more expensive, this tour company offers superb experiences. The company plans every facet of the travel for a single price. The common thread of both these trips was the imagination and creativity involved in providing access to the hidden gems of each place we travelled, again, the insider's view.

South America: We took a 22-day tour of South America with Globus. It was by far the most well organized tour we had ever taken, it was like we had planned it, mapping out the places we wanted to see, imagining the before and after. This bird's eye view of the tour started from *Manaus* which is on the banks of the

Negro river in northwestern Brazil. It is also the major departure point for the surrounding Amazon Rain Forest. Although we did not visit the deeper parts of the Amazon, we did take a boat tour through the dark *Negro river* to see the convergence with the muddy white *Silimoes River* resulting in the striking visual phenomenon called the "Meeting of the waters." These two rivers combine to form the Amazon River. Our tour guide on the boat gave us a recognition smile. We wondered if he recognized us as brown skinned tourists who had similar looks like him. Later as we talked, and he told us that he had great ambition to visit the Amazon forests as a young boy. He arrived in Manaus illegally when we was young and worked on the boats and traveled through the Amazon forests innumerable times. He had made it his home and settled there, the murky, black, white, ying and yang waters found him you could say, but the mix of light and dark was what he found.

Our tour guide was born in Chile, immigrated to the USA and lived in Miami for many years. To accompany tourists on this tour was his passion. He knew ins and outs of each place, and he took personal interest in each person on the tours. When we told him about our vegetarian food choice, he took it very seriously to find us different options on each day. Prior to us arriving at each restaurant the waiter seemed to know that we were vegetarians and had a special menu (7 courses) exactly like our other travel companions. We hardly noticed this was the longest tour we had taken. It was a dream.

Our next destination was Rio de Janeiro by bus. We traveled along the coastal beaches to magnificent water falls. The amazing 38m statue of *Crist the Redeemer* atop Corcovado Mountain was the highlight of the trip.

Our hotel overlooked the Pacific Ocean on one side and mountains on the other side. It was amazing to learn that a number of houses we were admiring all along the mountains belonged to the poor who were provided housing by the government. We walked along the beach in spite of receiving warnings that pickpockets were in abundance along the beach. We did not meet any such people. We were also invited to visit the factory of semi-precious stones. We had not seen such beautiful Tanzanite jewelry. We purchased an unusual watch which had its face made from the tanzanite dust. I gave it as a gift to my daughter-in-law, Rupa when my son Viral married her.

Iguazu National Park is the home of the magnificent waterfall. *Iguazu Falls is* located on the border of Brazil and Argentina, another crossroads. Our hotel was located in the park and was a short walking distance away from this incredible natural beauty. Iguazu Falls are twice as wide as the Niagara Falls and called as the "New Seven Wonders of the world by the New Seven Wonders of the World Foundation" in 2011. Our tour traveled from Brazil to Argentina to get a complete look at this falls. We walked along the Catwalks on the Brazilian side as well as on the Argentinian side to fully appreciate its horse shoe shape and the thundering waters of the Iguazu River. The falls change its colors at every hour of the day and in every season and both sides afford a different panorama.

Most impressive cultural scene was dancing; it was by far the South American rhythm that captivated us. *The Tango*, which originated in *Buenos Aires*, is the melancholy traditional dance while *Samba* is the Brazilian sensual cousin. We knew that we were in the world's greatest music destinations. The tour guide told us stories about the origins of Tango and Samba. The newly emigrated people from Spain as well as other European countries were downtrodden and lonely. They shared the music of their different cultures. Samba has African roots in tribal communities and it is performed by rhythmic belly dancers.

In Buenos Aires, our tour took us to a private *gaucho fiesta* where the cowboys of Argentina demonstrated their amazing riding and horse whispering skills, which also include an impressive array of acrobatic riding, herding, ring racing and horse dancing. It is no wonder Argentina has the best polo players in the world.

The next part of the tour was to the mystical, end-of-the-world *Patagonian landscape*. It is located at the southern tip of South America where Argentina meets Chile. I bought a blue Patagonia jacket in memory of its unbelievable beauty. To this date, I carry that jacket with me on my tours.

We proceeded to *Santiago, Chile*. My memory goes back to our walk along the main street where statues of world leaders who fought for peace were located. One of the statues was of Mahatma Gandhi who led a peaceful fight for the independence of India from the British Empire. It was a touching moment to see his statue on far away continent again.

Our last destination was *Peru*, where we spent time in *Lima, Cusco and Machu Picchu*. Cusco was the capital of the *Incan Empire*. We took a train from Cusco to Machu Picchu. The description of the train's ascent in the *Andes* was too special not to share, so I emailed our children, knowing fully that on the train in the mountains on our way to Machu Picchu there were no chances that the email will reach them in New York. Internet was not commonly available at that time. But I felt good writing about it. To my total surprise our daughter responded in five minutes. On one hand we were in the Lost City of the Incas, discovered in 1911, standing 8,000 feet above the sea level communicating with our children walking the sleepless streets of New York. Technology can amaze. *Machu Picchu was recently named one of the New Seven Wonders of the World"*. Its walls, terraces, and ramps work in harmony with their mountainous surroundings. This site was a tribute to the creativity and skills of the Incas. It is a citadel built at the peak of the Incan civilization on top of the Andes mountain peak. Its intricate stonework defies modern age architectures.

We visited the Choco Museo and watched the natives teach

a chocolate making class. We also visited a local *alpaca and llama farm* where these animals are raised. They both are from the Andean Mountains of Peru, Chile and Bolivia of South America. They produce luxury fiber, unusually strong and its superior quality makes fine finished garments. I bought two skirts and two sweaters which have become permanent parts of my wardrobe.

Viren and Nalini at Ankorwat, the largest Religious
Monument in the world, Siem Reap, Cambodia

Meeting of waters of two rivers, dark water of Rio
Negro and white water of Rio Silimoes to form River
Amazon in Manaus, Brazil, South America

Iguazu Falls, Argentinian side, South America

Viren and Nalini with our tour guide in South America

Patagonia, the southernmost tip of South America

Viren and Nalini in Machu Picchu, Peru, South America

Viren and Nalini at Corovado Mountain to watch the
statue of Christ the Redeemer in Rio De Jeniero, Brazil

A Room with a View

Waking up to an expansive panorama, ocean or a beach horizon, magnanimous falls, where sunrise or sunset can be viewed, where open forest, grazing animals or remarkable monuments can be viewed has been my definition of a beautiful room. I have stayed at numerous hotels and motels during my travels (63 nights a year for 12 years); however the most memorable ones are those where my request to be on a higher floor in a room where there was a view from my window was granted by the front desk. I compromised on the kind of bed (Double, Queen or a King sized bed) I would get, only for the view.

The view from my balcony of the hotel in Dalhousie, India, I could see the towering Himalayas. Nature has a special grasp on my psyche. Watching the beauty of nature is the most satisfying thing I have had in my travels. I get mesmerized and lost in the vastness of nature.

On our tour to the Canadian Rockies we had a hotel with a view from the Fairmont Chateau Lake Louise. I truly felt I was in heaven. The turquois color of the water of Lake Louise is so unique and pristine that I could not stop taking the view with me through the lens of my camera.

In the United States on one of my psychiatric conferences, I stayed at a hotel in Toronto where my window opened to the Roger Stadium where Blue Jays (Baseball team) played at home. This was an unusual but amazingly pleasurable view from my hotel room. We watched all three games that Blue Jays played at home; an experience all in one!

At Niagara Falls in Canada, my room overlooked the entire falls. The chairs in our room faced the large ceiling to the floor window of our hotel room. I had no need to sleep but to get absorbed in this natural beauty.

My hotel rooms at a higher floor have also provided me opportunities to watch the most amazing sunrises and sunsets. They fascinate me. There is a different view every minute.

I have stayed in rooms with balconies that overlook the beach and the ocean. It is an amazing experience to sit out in the balcony, get mesmerized while watching the tides and the waves.

Our journey to the Antarctica by cruise was truly captivating. We had a corner room at the tail end of the ship. It had windows on two sides. The sheer majesty of ice and the unique wildlife was extraordinary to watch. The primary reason to visit Antarctica was to watch the Penguins. From our cabin we saw them as black spots on pristine white ice. When I approached them it was impossible to take my eyes away from them. Ever since I watched penguins in Australia, I was determined to visit Antarctica. To this day, it remains one of the best natural continent where only researchers stay for certain period of time.

It is a real joy to share my travel experiences with my children and my husband if he was not traveling with me. Since the advent of Internet availability during all my recent travels, I have captured such views from my windows on iPhone camera and sent them to my loved ones. It is a powerful way to build family bonds and create memories of a lifetime.

It has also broadened my awareness and appreciation of world's diverse cultures, natural beauty, cuisines and its wild life.

We have travelled to all seven continents of the world by motor coaches and cars on land, cruise ships in the sea and river and by planes to reach faraway lands. Many of these travels have been solo since I had a travelling job. Many of these travels were with my husband, some with all three children, some with friends, and some on organized tours. There has been real world learning and fun that has built bonds across the generations. Each of these travels has been compelling and inspirational. I have learned that how we see the world matters. After all, travel is all about stories we hear and about things we see, people we meet and make connections and the memories we keep in our hearts

Another such place is Hotel Del Coronado, located in Coronado, California. The closest airport is San Diego airport. It is connected with San Diego by a bridge. It is a national treasure, as the oldest completely wood hotel built in 1888. It has cottages and villas, all identified by red roof. It has the top beaches in the US. It owns 28 acres of land and offers year round activities. Every evening one can watch the spectacular sunset.

In 1885, two businessmen, Hancock and Hampton came to this area and identified the site where Hotel Del Coronado would go up. US presidents, Taft, Benjamin Harrison, Nixon, Johnson, Regan, and Clinton have lived here. Thomas Edison, Charles Lindbergh, Babe Ruth are some of the other celebrities who stayed here. King of Hawaii, in 1891 spent Christmas here, Prince of Wales; Edward married Wallace Simpson who lived in Coronado. He gave up his throne to marry her.

Hotel Del Coronado played a role during World War II. As a civilian hotel it served the serviceman who lived here and some married and spent their honeymoon here as well. Kate Morgan, in 1891 killed herself in this hotel when her lover did not show up for a date in the hotel. The locals say that she lives in the hotel as a ghost and she is known as a *"Beautiful Stranger."* Al Frank Baum, author of *Wizard of Oz* lived here.

Hollywood stars, Steven Spielberg, Charlie Chaplin, Clark Gable, Jane Russel, Cary Grant, Mickey Rooney, Catherine Hepburn, Frank Sinatra, Jack Lemon, Brad Pitt, Jody Foster,

Michele Pfeiffer and Madonna have visited here as well. Marilyn Monroe's movie *"Some Like it Hot"* was filmed here. In addition to the celebrities, this incredible hotel has attracted vacationers from all over the world for more than 125 years.

I was very fortunate to have stayed here for two nights. The room rates range from $300-2000. I had a beautiful balcony partly overlooking the Pacific Ocean and partly the swimming pools and the gardens. There is a beautiful boardwalk, which is used all year round. I sat and watched the waves of the ocean from my balcony and also watched the sun set each night before going out for dinner.

Baseball Field from our hotel room, Toronto, Canada

Sunset from the balcony of our hotel room

View from my room

View from my room

View from my room

View from my hotel room, Dubrovnik, Croatia

Lone Traveling

Although I have not traveled alone for solely pleasure, my job related travels are solo. Although I love to travel with my, husband, children and friends, traveling alone is perhaps the best way to get to know you.

Needless to say that traveling alone has built in fear of navigating the unknown. I have always known that travels have helped me recover from empty nest syndrome after each child left home for college. It has provided me spiritual answers for finding a purpose in life and just an escape from a mundane routine. However, going solo for my job was challenging to start and became habit-forming and almost addictively enjoyable as time passed.

I learned that alone time is healthy. It has been a voyage of self-discovery and self-knowledge. It has been refreshing to reflect and reexamine the direction life is taking. It is also a perfect time to focus on new direction and a new goal. Some distance from people has helped me realize which people are important and which ones produce negative energy.

In my job related travels I have visited universities and large academic medical centers in large cities to smaller ones located in distant parts of the country. I find myself more in tuned with my surroundings. I notice the unique characteristics of people. I engage in conversations with taxi drivers that drive me from airport to hotels and from hotels to the institutions. In the most remote places I have been the darkest person in the institution and certainly a person who speaks English with an accent. However, many of my conversations are heartfelt that leave behind an impression.

I have spent an afternoon sometimes lingering in places that the town boasts about. For instance, Glass Museum in Toledo, Ohio, Baseball hall of fame in Cooperstown, NY, Basketball Hall of Fame in Springfield, MA, National Museum of the US Air Force in Dayton, Ohio, Horse Race Derby in Lexington, Kentucky, wandering in Reading Terminal Market in Philadelphia, Walking in Times Square in Manhattan, NY, Louisville Slugger Museum and Factory to name just a few.

I loved the way I felt every time I traveled alone. It had my own story which was deeper and the memory has lasted longer. I have learned to overcome loneliness and I have developed a new attitude toward loneliness. Solo traveling has taught me perspective and patience, how to deal with stress and how to interact socially with people from different cultures, and demographics. I have learned to refrain from judging people. I have learned to keep an open mind, chat with people with common interests but always keeping safety in mind.

In my earlier days of solo travels, I was uncomfortable and conscious of eating alone in a restaurant. But as time passed, I felt a sense of empowerment. I did not sit with my back facing the entrance to the restaurant and hiding my face in a newspaper, a book or recently my iPhone. I sit facing the entrance of the restaurant, and with a smile say to the lady who sits me that I need a table for one. My next challenge was to explain to the waiter that I am a vegetarian and ask for all the condiments, which would make my food tasty. I have become more observant, curious, details oriented without making judgments.

My attitude of smiling while keeping my guards up has worked well with me. My personal discipline is to learn from the locals, not to go outside at night and be aware of my surrounding.

An older woman in a store where I was shopping in the French Quarters in New Orleans asked me if I was traveling alone. When I answered in affirmative, she said that decent single women do not roam around this area after dark. I went back to the hotel and started to ask people why I was given that tip. I was told by the locals reluctantly that prostitutes were out roaming the area after dark. This older woman was looking out for my safety. Traveling alone has forced me to step out of my comfort zone and meet new people. I have made incredible bonds with new people who I may have known only for a few hours but remember them for years to come. Email contacts and Facebook have certainly helped.

I enjoy the sunrise and sunsets from my higher floor windows of the hotels which I request on my every visit. I have innumerable pictures shot out of my window. It is an incredible feeling to witness that no sunrise or sunset is exactly alike.

Future in Traveling

As long as I am physically and mentally able, I hope to travel. There are new sites and experiences waiting to be seen. I have some places already in my bucket list. The list of exploring, learning and enjoying the people, the places and above all the nature can never end. As my energy level goes down, my travels may also slow down but I have my memory bank to visit frequently, tons of pictures to watch and walk down the memory lane over and over again. In near future my desire is to visit two of the world's most pristine environments; Salar de Uyuni and Atacama Desert. I can visualize traveling from the peaks of the Andes to the majestic Salt Flats of Bolivia in central-south America. This is where the Salar turns into a virtual mirror. This impressive area of the world is the best place for incredible snap shots. Although I tend to travel in comfort, this will be a place where I am willing to take some discomforts.

Robert Hutchins Goddard once said, "It is difficult to say what is impossible, for the dream of yesterday is the hope of today and reality of tomorrow." I will always push on.

When I think about future in travels, I realize that life is a journey. I believe in previous lives and previous journeys with each one interconnected. I have met loved ones as well as strangers on this journey in this life and somewhere in previous lives as well. My experiences are also interconnected. This journey of travels will continue until "Nirvana." A state of Bliss that I enter every time I travel.

Final Words

I hope that I have become a better person, a reasonable person who appreciates life. I have learned to be more empathetic, compassionate and patient. I can attribute this to my travels, and I hope if anything comes from this read, it is that I hope I have inspired you to see something else, go beyond your comfort zone, and explore a differently vibrant world. Life is a journey which we begin alone and will end alone. Experiences are all gathered in this life in its various phases. It is an incredibly fulfilling and gratifying feeling that words cannot describe. Despite that, I hope my words have described my travels, what I learned, and ultimately, inspired you to stand up––and see the world.

Inspiration from my Travels

Author Nalini Juthani left India for the United States in June of 1970. Her mission was to get higher education and travel the world. She has fulfilled her dreams of traveling through all seven continents of the world and enhanced her life by creating such travel experiences. In this memoir, *"Inspiration from my Travels"*, the author shares enriching travel experiences that has inspired her. She inspires the readers to write their own memoir and leave a legacy for the next generation.

After leaving her homeland India, she became a naturalized citizen of America, raised children and grandchildren in America, lived a fulfilling professional and personal life in her adoptive land and made it her new home. However, this transition did not occur without an emotional turmoil. Through her travels she explored and learned a great deal about what was "Home" and what did feeling like a "Foreigner" in both lands really mean!

These essays with photographs included, provide a glimpse of her travels through all seven continents of the world starting from within India. *"Inspiration from my Travels"* narrates her experiences of travels with her husband, children, friends, and as a lone traveler.

Inspiring and touching, the essays describe the influence Juthani had on the lives of people she met during her travels while overcoming cultural barriers and dietary restrictions as a vegetarian that she had to overcome to travel outside the confines of her protective environment.